ALWAYS A BRIDESMAID

BY JESSIE JONES
NICHOLAS HOPE
JAMIE WOOTEN

★

★

DRAMATISTS
PLAY SERVICE
INC.

ALWAYS A BRIDESMAID
Copyright © 2013, Jessie Jones, Nicholas Hope, Jamie Wooten

All Rights Reserved

CAUTION: Professionals and amateurs are hereby warned that performance of ALWAYS A BRIDESMAID is subject to payment of a royalty. It is fully protected under the copyright laws of the United States of America, and of all countries covered by the International Copyright Union (including the Dominion of Canada and the rest of the British Commonwealth), and of all countries covered by the Pan-American Copyright Convention, the Universal Copyright Convention, the Berne Convention, and of all countries with which the United States has reciprocal copyright relations. All rights, including without limitation professional/amateur stage rights, motion picture, recitation, lecturing, public reading, radio broadcasting, television, video or sound recording, all other forms of mechanical, electronic and digital reproduction, transmission and distribution, such as CD, DVD, the Internet, private and file-sharing networks, information storage and retrieval systems, photocopying, and the rights of translation into foreign languages are strictly reserved. Particular emphasis is placed upon the matter of readings, permission for which must be secured from the Authors' agent in writing.

The English language stock and amateur stage performance rights in the United States, its territories, possessions and Canada for ALWAYS A BRIDESMAID are controlled exclusively by DRAMATISTS PLAY SERVICE, INC., 440 Park Avenue South, New York, NY 10016. No professional or nonprofessional performance of the Play may be given without obtaining in advance the written permission of DRAMATISTS PLAY SERVICE, INC., and paying the requisite fee.

Inquiries concerning all other rights should be addressed to the Authors c/o Dramatists Play Service, 440 Park Avenue South, New York, NY 10016.

SPECIAL NOTE
Anyone receiving permission to produce ALWAYS A BRIDESMAID is required to give credit to the Authors as sole and exclusive Authors of the Play on the title page of all programs distributed in connection with performances of the Play and in all instances in which the title of the Play appears for purposes of advertising, publicizing or otherwise exploiting the Play and/or a production thereof. The names of the Authors must appear on a separate line, in which no other name appears, immediately beneath the title and in size of type equal to 50% of the size of the largest, most prominent letter used for the title of the Play. No person, firm or entity may receive credit larger or more prominent than that accorded the Authors.

SPECIAL NOTE ON LOGO
The logo for ALWAYS A BRIDESMAID, available for download at www.dramatists.com, is required for use in all playbills, posters and other promotional materials.

*This play is dedicated to our Twink, our Nita, our Beth …
our friend, Kerry Shannon.*

AUTHORS' NOTES

The name "Kari" should be pronounced "CAR-ee."

The costumes in this play are an integral part of the comedy. Therefore great care and specificity should be taken in selecting and/or constructing each of them.

We suggest the pace of the play — and scene transitions — be brisk and lively.

We suggest thematic up-tempo music concerning love, weddings, romance, etc., be played pre- and post-show, at intermission and especially during scene transitions.

All of the characters portrayed in ALWAYS A BRIDESMAID are fictional creations and any resemblance to real persons, living or dead, is purely coincidental.

ALWAYS A BRIDESMAID received its world premiere at Grapevine's Runway Theatre in Grapevine, Texas, on April 5, 2013. It was directed by Kenny Green; the assistant director/stage manager was Russell Sebastian; the set design was by Ellen Mizener; the sound design was by Jeff Mizener; the costume coordination was by Misty Baptiste; the property coordination was by Traci Clements; and the original Jones Hope Wooten show logo was designed by Joe Connor. The cast was as follows:

KARI AMES-BISSETTE	Kelly Kennedy
LIBBY RUTH AMES	Patsy Hester Daussat
SEDALIA ELLICOTT	Sue Ellen Love
MONETTE GENTRY	Dana Harrison
CHARLIE COLLINS	Dena Dunn
DEEDRA WINGATE	Connie Lane

CHARACTERS
(in order of appearance)

KARI AMES-BISSETTE, late 20s, a kind-hearted, spirited Southern charmer

LIBBY RUTH AMES, late 40s, hopeless romantic, sweet country woman, plain-spoken and guileless

SEDALIA ELLICOTT, 60s, a gregarious, energetic Virginia hostess and life-force

MONETTE GENTRY, late 40s, kinda flashy, kinda trashy, Southern-to-the-bone flirt

CHARLIE COLLINS, late 40s, tree-hugging, Birkenstock-wearing, acerbic Southern free spirit

DEEDRA WINGATE, late 40s, headstrong with a dry wit, no-nonsense Northern transplant

PLACE

An upstairs sitting room at historic Laurelton Oaks, Laurelton, Virginia, twenty miles northwest of Richmond

TIME

The play takes place over a period of seven years.

ACT ONE

Scene 1: A Spring afternoon
Scene 2: A Summer afternoon, two years later

ACT TWO

Scene 1: A Fall evening, four years later
Scene 2: A Winter afternoon, one year later

ALWAYS A BRIDESMAID

ACT ONE

Scene 1

A light comes up downstage right on Kari Ames-Bissette, late 20s, dressed in a beautiful bridal gown. Facing the audience, she taps a spoon against her champagne flute, stops and excitedly addresses "the guests at her wedding."

KARI. *(Lively, upbeat.)* Hello! Can you hear me? I'd hate for y'all to *miss* my first official moment as a *Mrs. (Giggles.)* … On behalf of myself and Todd, my *husband — dang*, I like the sound of *that (Sighs happily.)* … I want to thank all of you for being here on this wonderful day. We've all come together in this beautiful setting to celebrate *love*. And speaking of which, I want to thank my Aunt Viola who was so sweet to reduce the restraining order against Uncle Huell to thirty feet so he could also be in this room with us today. That was just so generous of — *(Her attention caught, stern.)* Uncle Huell, get back! You hug that wall! We are not going to have a repeat of that ugly mess you made of Easter Sunday! *(Beat.)* That's better. *(Then, to the "guests," sweetly.)* Now, wasn't the ceremony just precious?! And that little Brandon is a trouper — four years old and his very first time to be a ring-bearer. Shoot, under that kind of pressure, I would've thrown up, too. But he's fine now and the photographer promised to delete all those pictures. And Todd and I absolutely insist on picking up the dry cleaning bill for everyone who was seated at the end of row four. Oh, and those doves! They were awesome! The image of them being released and soaring into the sky the moment Todd and I kissed will always stay

with me … even though it might have ended better if someone had remembered today *is* the first day of hunting season. *(Louder.)* And I've been assured our ears will stop ringing from the gunfire before the first dance. *(Sips champagne.)* I'm not much of a drinker, but I *do* like *this! (Laughs.)* Now, I have some people to thank — Daddy, of course, for his love and generosity and my mom and her best friends, my godmothers, for teaching me everything they know about how to survive "The Big Day." Actually, at one of *their* weddings, six, maybe seven years ago right here at Laurelton Oaks, I learned lesson number one: expect the unexpected. There's an old saying: "If you want to make God laugh, tell him your plans." Well, I found out *that* day if you really want to make him double over and howl, tell him your *wedding* plans! *(Laughs, sips. Cross fade, lights down on Kari as they come up center stage on an elegantly appointed upstairs sitting room at Laurelton Oaks, a stately Virginia home that's been converted into an upscale events venue. It's a spring afternoon. Upstage right is a door to a dressing room. Upstage left is a door to another dressing room. Downstage right an upholstered stool sits in front of a small dressing table that is littered with makeup. Against the upstage center wall is a decorative chest on which a lamp, an opened bottle of champagne and flutes have been placed. Several shopping bags are on the floor nearby. A painting hangs above the chest. Downstage center is a small sofa that has a large purse on it. A pretty upholstered chair sits on either side of the sofa. On the downstage left wall is the door to the hallway, further downstage left is an occasional table that holds a small floral arrangement, a chair next to it. Libby Ruth Ames, late 40s, in a rather dowdy, floor-length coral-colored dress and matching jacket, stands at an ironing board, presses the bottom of her own skirt and sings a lively, off-key country rendition of "Oh, Promise Me." She sways in time as she irons the skirt and rhythmically squirts it with a spray bottle as she sings.*
LIBBY RUTH. *(Sings, passionately.)* OH, PROMISE ME THAT SOME DAY YOU AND I *(Squirt, squirt, squirt.)* WILL TAKE OUR LOVE TOGETHER TO SOME SKY *(Squirt, squirt, squirt. Sedalia Ellicott, 60s, in a dramatic caftan and ropes of pearls, charges into the room, stops as Libby Ruth belts the final, off-key note, big finish.)* OH, PROMISE ME, OH, PROOOMISE *ME!!! (Sedalia winces.)*
SEDALIA. Libby Ruth, not to squat on your enthusiasm, darlin', but I've got a reception hall *full* of delicate crystal. You hit any more jackhammer notes like that, and our guests will be sippin' champagne out of Dixie cups.

LIBBY RUTH. *(Laughs, resumes ironing.)* I'm sorry. Preston always tells me I sound like a herd of cats fightin' over a bagpipe but I get carried away. That's just me, hopeless romantic! Look, I know this wedding came out of the blue, how can I ever thank you for squeezing Monette in this afternoon?
SEDALIA. Well, other than swearin' not to sing anymore, absolutely nothing. Here at Laurelton Oaks, we're flexible. It comes from decades of experience hosting elegant celebrations for a refined clientele– *(Monette Gentry, 40s, enters from the upstage right dressing room in a deeply revealing white lace slip, several rollers in her hair, grabs her purse from the sofa, rummages through it.)*
MONETTE. I am gonna find those blasted tweezers even if I have to tear up the joint and cold cock everyone in the room to do it! *(Storms out upstage right dressing room door.)*
LIBBY RUTH. *(To Sedalia.)* Which is why we appreciate you makin' an exception for *us*. *(Monette screams offstage, then rushes back into the room.)*
MONETTE. I just caught sight of my butt in that full-length mirror! *(Whirls around, sticks out her rear.)* Look at it! *(Slaps it.)* You could show IMAX movies on this thing! *(Groans, hurries out upstage right dressing room door.)*
LIBBY RUTH. A *really big* exception. *(Then, low.)* Listen, Sedalia, truth is, Monette's marrying a younger man and she's feeling a little pressured. She told me she's only got half an hour to lose fifteen pounds! And to that end, I may need your help squeezing her into that third pair of Spanx.
SEDALIA. You know, there *is* one thing I find curious: in all my years doing this, I've found that most of my ... shall we say, *mature* brides — particularly those who've made that long walk *before* — tend to go for simple wedding ceremonies, with maybe just one attendant, if any. I was surprised your friend chose to have *three*.
LIBBY RUTH. Yes, I'm sure it does seem a little odd. But see, we were all best friends as kids and we made a promise that we'd be in each others' weddings, no matter what. And we did that. But about ten years ago when Monette married the second time, she asked us to stand up for her *again* and we did ... *again*. And this time, well ... I think she's startin' to look on this as a kind of tradition.
SEDALIA. I see. That's nice ... a little weird, but ... nice.
LIBBY RUTH. Yeah ... we think so, too. *(From offstage, Monette*

yelps, frustrated.) Monette's a little intense today, but she always is right before she vows to love some guy forever.
SEDALIA.   Don't worry, Libby Ruth, I've seen it all: nervous brides, nauseous brides, blushing brides, belligerent brides and brides having contractions three minutes apart. I can handle intensity. *(Unseen, Monette enters from the upstage right dressing room door with a mirror and tweezers, works on her eyebrows.)* And should this *tradition* continue, you might want to pass this info along to your friend: here at the Oaks we offer a customer loyalty discount in the event the need arises for any … *future nuptials.*
MONETTE.   *(Snaps to attention.)* What are you insinuating, Ms. Ellicott? That just because I've struck out with two previous husbands, I might not be able to hang onto Number Three? What have you said to her, Libby Ruth? 'Cause I'm here to tell you, marrying right out of high school can't be held against me. It was six of the best weeks of my life until Trey violated his parole. And of course my marriage to Vince bit the dust when I found out he'd been putting on my dresses and hitting the clubs every time I went out of town on business. Why I wasn't suspicious when he bought me so many *oversized* lace panties is beyond me. But the past is the past and that trash is burned! This is *today* and come hell or high water, I am marrying Gavin Reed. This guy's *the one!*
SEDALIA.   *(Unruffled.)* I'm only saying repeat clients get *twenty percent* off any subsequent weddings. *(Offers a business card.)*
MONETTE.   Wow, that *is* a nice discount. *(Tucks the card into her décolletage.)* Better safe than sorry. *(Hurriedly exits upstage right dressing room door.)*
SEDALIA.   Now, I don't want Monette to feel like she's getting the bum's rush, but we need to keep the ball rolling this afternoon. *(Crosses upstage, fills a champagne flute.)* I've got a great big event starting at six. Effie Gudger's turning one hundred and if that old bird's still suckin' wind after I've served up the birthday puddin', I'm calling the whole wing-ding a success.
LIBBY RUTH.   Oh, we'll be ready; we're only missing one bridesmaid. And Monette understands, she's a businesswoman, too. Did you know that she owns the biggest country music club in the entire state of Virginia?
SEDALIA.   A successful businesswoman. Hmm. I may have underestimated her.
MONETTE.   *(Calls offstage.)* Libby Ruth, do you think this jack-

et's so low cut it's going to show my Harley tattoo?
SEDALIA. On second thought, I believe I nailed it.
LIBBY RUTH. *(Re: champagne flute.)* You always think of the nicest touches. Maybe I'll take that champagne to Monette now.
SEDALIA. Monette? Darlin', how do you think I get through all these joyful occasions? *(Gulps it.)* The bride's on her own. *(Exits downstage left hallway door.)*
LIBBY RUTH. *(Dreamy.)* I love weddings, everybody so happy, and feelin' good! *(Just then, Charlie Collins, 40s, dressed in an oddly-put-together, pink-ish pants outfit and Birkenstock sandals, her hair a mess, steps out of the upstage left door, drapes herself against the frame, has a terrible cold.)*
CHARLIE. Is it time to drag what's left of me down the aisle? *(Sneezes.)*
LIBBY RUTH. Charlie, your cold is worse! *(Low.)* We can't let Monette know you're sick 'til we *have* to. She's already got herself wound so tight today she's liable to stroke out. She'll never forgive us if she has to honeymoon in the E.R.
CHARLIE. Like it's not hard enough for us single gals to witness these lovey-dovey, bless-ed nuptials without wanting to run screaming into the hills. Nooo, I have to go and get the crud on top of it so I can enjoy it *even more*. And why is this such a rush job, anyway?
LIBBY RUTH. That's just Monette. When it comes to men, she throws herself headlong at the one she wants. *(Low.)* If you ask me, I think she's scared if she doesn't grab him, she'll lose him forever and for Monette, that would be tragic. *(Studies Charlie.)* Kind of like your hair. Oh, for heaven's sake, sit down here and let me take a shot at that mess. I can't stand to see you lookin' so pitiful. *(Charlie plops into the chair stage left of the sofa. Libby Ruth works on her hair.)*
CHARLIE. You know, there are three constants in my life — taxes I can barely pay, recurring bladder infections and being a bridesmaid in a Monette Gentry wedding. She goes through husbands like Sherman through Georgia and I can't even get *one* sucker down the aisle.
LIBBY RUTH. But what happened to that last guy you were dating? He didn't seem to mind that you spend your life diggin' in the dirt or that you've got the fashion sense of a color-blind prison guard or even that every food this side of melba toast makes you extra gassy. I thought he was really into you.
CHARLIE. What he was *really* into was identity theft. Once I dis-

covered he'd stolen my credit cards, I pressed charges and that pretty much put the kay-bosh on our little love-fest. I honestly don't get why I have this rotten luck with men. I'm not looking for a sugar daddy, I own my own home, I … Ah … Ah … *(Sneezes loudly, rubs a tissue all over her nose and face).* I mean, I'm a real catch, right?
LIBBY RUTH. Well … maybe not at this exact moment.
CHARLIE. It's not that I don't meet lots of men through my landscaping business, I do. But it feels like every whack job with a backhoe is drawn to me like a dog to a tree stump. When did I become a *freak* magnet?! I just want to meet a nice guy who hates the same stuff as me.
LIBBY RUTH. Same thing's happening with Kari. My little girl's downstairs right now moping around because she and her boyfriend broke up. The two of you just need to believe that you'll find your true love one day when you least expect it.
CHARLIE. I don't need love to take me by surprise. How about Thursday night, eight o'clock? *(Hit by a coughing fit, hurries out upstage left dressing room door.)*
LIBBY RUTH. *(Calls to her.)* Turn on the hot water and breathe the steam but don't let Monette catch you at it. And take another shot at that hair! *(Monette enters from the upstage right dressing room, adjusts the skirt of her bridal suit.)*
MONETTE. Aren't we starting soon? Where on earth are Deedra and Charlie?
LIBBY RUTH. Oh, um … *(Covers.)* Charlie's here. She's got a little tickle in her throat, so she's resting in the other dressing room. But no word yet from Deedra.
MONETTE. Well, she better hurry up and get here. None of us has ever missed one of our weddings yet. *(Checks herself in the mirror. Sighs.)* God, I'd do *anything* to be thin — except diet or exercise.
LIBBY RUTH. Monette, as usual, you make a beautiful bride. Hey, remember when we were growing up, the four of us would sit in the field across the road and daydream about getting married in a gorgeous old house like Laurelton Oaks? Well, today you're making that dream come true! And it's all just so romantic! *(Hugs her. Then pulls back.)* Although it is a little *unusual* that none of us has even met *this* groom or know anything about him!
MONETTE. *(Removes rollers from her hair.)* Oh. Okay, what can I tell you?

LIBBY RUTH. Well, I'm always fascinated by what makes people fall in love. Like when I first met Preston, all I saw were those sparkling eyes and that dimple in his chin and I was a *goner*. Of course, I'd just rear-ended his new truck and the veins in his neck were bulging and he was screaming, but for me it was love at first sight. Oh, golly, now I laugh about how we met … he still can't, but I do. So, what was it that first attracted you to Calvin?
MONETTE. It's Gavin! *(Crosses downstage center.)* Okay, come here. *(Libby Ruth hurries to join her, facing the audience at the "window" that overlooks a rose garden. Monette points.)* You see that unbelievably nervous guy down there?
LIBBY RUTH. The one who just dropped his keys?
MONETTE. Yep. Now, wait … he's bending over to pick them up and … there!
LIBBY RUTH. Oh. *(Enjoys the view.) Ohhhh, my*!
MONETTE. And when I found out he sits that cute butt of his in the heated leather seat of a cute little Porsche, I absolutely *had* to know more about the man! Isn't he a doll?! He's so smart and we talk for hours. And he finds me fascinating — which is an attribute I absolutely insist on in a husband. Gavin's in advertising, he makes his own pasta, works out six times a week … *(Carried away.)* has the biceps of a Greek god … *(Ecstatic.)* … and on our second date he *rewired the lamps in my living room … (Fans herself. Libby Ruth grabs the spray bottle off the ironing board.)* … Did I mention he likes to garden … *with his shirt off?!! (Libby Ruth spritzes her several times.)*
LIBBY RUTH. Alright, let's just cool it down, girlfriend. We've got to get you through this ceremony without weirding out the minister.
MONETTE. *(Calms down.)* Okay, I'm good, I'm back. I'll go dry off and trowel on some more paint. *(Quickly exits upstage right dressing room door.)*
LIBBY RUTH. *(To herself.)* That woman is hotter than a bucket of jalapeños! It'll be a miracle if we can keep her from starting the honeymoon *before* they finish the "I do's." *(Charlie enters from upstage left dressing room, with a large box of tissues, her hair is wild, a large brush stuck in it.)*
CHARLIE. *(Re: hair.)* It started out okay, but somewhere it went horribly wrong.
LIBBY RUTH. Oh, no! What have you done?! There's no way in the world you could've made this any worse! *(Monette, now in her*

sexy, form-fitting and cleavage-revealing jacket, races in from upstage right dressing room.)
MONETTE. Are my eyebrows too — *(Charlie sneezes, Monette freezes.)* Noooo! Libby Ruth, you said she had a tickle in her throat! She's sick as a dog!
CHARLIE. Good to see you, too, Monette. Congrats on reeling in another one.
MONETTE. Get out of here! In less than an hour I'm leaving for Jamaica with the gorgeous hunk of my dreams and you, Charlene Beatrice Collins, are not going to ruin it by giving me your slimy, snotty cold! What do you think you're doing?!
CHARLIE. I *believe* I'm keeping the promise we made a hundred years ago that we'd be in each others' weddings. But I had no idea this was going to be a regular gig for the rest of my life. It's like a bad student loan I can never pay off.
LIBBY RUTH. Now, get a hold of yourself, Monette. Remember, Charlie *has* been there for every single one of our weddings. Just like we'll be there for hers.
CHARLIE. Which will be the day after world peace is declared and Elvis has risen from the dead. Mark your calendars.
MONETTE. *(Pouts.)* Alright, fine. Just don't breathe on me, Charlie. *(Grabs a tissue, holds it over her nose and mouth.)* Fix that hair and don't touch anything! I don't want any of your cooties! *(Notices Charlie's clothes. Gasps.)* And you're wearing pants … *(Gasps.)* and *Birkenstocks?!* Listen to me: you cannot participate in this event wearing your normal "earth-nugget" get-up. Hug a tree some other time! Right now you need to be in a cocktail length dress!
CHARLIE. You gave us less than twenty-four hours to rearrange our schedules and get here! And none of the ugly bridesmaids dresses from all the previous weddings the three of you have had were *coral*. I don't have a large inventory of girly dress-up crap, so it's *what you see* or total nudity. Either way, I'm good to go. I … Ah … Ah … *(Sneezes. Blows her nose loudly. The others recoil.)*
LIBBY RUTH. I'll get the Lysol! *(Exits upstage left dressing room door.)*
MONETTE. And I'll head off the plague at the source! *(Grabs a paper shopping bag, puts it over Charlie's head, races out upstage right dressing room door.)*
CHARLIE. Monette? Libby Ruth? Hello? Where did everybody — Ah … Ah … *(Sneezes tremendously. Beat. Disgusted.)* Oh, God.

(Libby Ruth sails in the upstage left dressing room door with Lysol and a cloth, does a double-take when she sees the bag, approaches Charlie, gingerly pats the top of the bag.)

LIBBY RUTH. Shug, isn't this is a little extreme? There's no shame in being sick. But Monette's kinda on edge, so let's be good, calm bridesmaids. We don't want anything else to happen that could upset her day. *(Just then, Deedra Wingate, 40s, bursts into the room. She wears casual khaki walking shorts and a short-sleeve white blouse.)*

DEEDRA. *(Rages.)* This is an outrage!! It's … it's absolutely absurd! *(Charlie takes the bag off her head.)*

CHARLIE. Can't fight you there, Deedra, but we promised Monette we'd be here, so let's woman up and get this fool for love down the aisle … again.

DEEDRA. I'm trying to tell you I've just been robbed! I stopped at our old drug store to pick up a lipstick and when I came out, some guy was running down Main Street with my stuff! What kind of man would break into a car and steal a makeup kit and a dress?

LIBBY RUTH. You know, Monette's second husband comes to mind. *(Monette enters from upstage right dressing room, fastens a string of pearls on her neck.)*

MONETTE. Deedra! Thank God you're here!

DEEDRA. Barely. A thief broke my window, stole my clothes, there's glass everywhere! It's a miracle I'm not cut to shreds. My blood pressure's sky high!

MONETTE. Good lord, Deedra! This is a *catastrophe!!* *(Re: Deedra's outfit.)* That's all you've got to wear in my wedding?!

DEEDRA. *(Dry.)* No really, I'm fine. And your deep concern for my well-being is so touching. It was selfish of me to go and make myself the victim of a violent crime. I swear it won't happen on your *next* wedding day.

MONETTE. *(Sweetly, begrudging.)* Well … that's more like it. *(Hugs Deedra.)*

CHARLIE. Come on, Deedra, people get robbed every day, but we only get to marry Monette off every decade or so.

DEEDRA. *(Takes a deep breath, slowly exhales.)* Look, I'm here, nobody died, I called the police, it's done. Besides, I hated that dress anyway. And I hope it makes that guy look *fat*.

LIBBY RUTH. See, everything's fine now! What matters is you're safe and we're together. We don't get to spend nearly enough time with each other, but when we do, we make it count!

DEEDRA. You're right. In fact, Charlie, I haven't seen *you* in forever. *(Opens her arms for a hug.)*
MONETTE. Don't touch her!
CHARLIE. Unless you're packing penicillin.
MONETTE. Look, Deedra, I really *do* appreciate what you went through to get here. That drive from D.C.'s a bear. And for a woman of your temperament, I know it must've been tough. *(Remembers something!)* Earrings! *(Hurries out upstage right dressing room door.)*
DEEDRA. What did she mean a "woman of my temperament"?
LIBBY RUTH. She meant it as a compliment. Honey, you have no patience, never have. You don't tolerate fools, liars or wasting time. But those are *good* qualities for a judge.
CHARLIE. Along with that scowl you've perfected.
DEEDRA. *(Frowns, miffed.)* What scowl?
LIBBY RUTH. You know, when you squinch up your face and — there! That one! No wonder criminals and small dogs are scared of you. But the three of us know way underneath you have a good heart. Took us some time to figure that out after you moved to Laurelton. 'Til tenth grade we just chalked up your *unique* personality to your being a foreign exchange student.
DEEDRA. I moved here from Connecticut.
LIBBY RUTH. And we never held it against you — treated you just like you were one of us.
DEEDRA. Okay, before any more of your compliments drive me downstairs into the bar, let's get me ready. But this side of a smile and a shower curtain, I'm fresh out of ideas of what to wear to this shindig. Anyone?
LIBBY RUTH. Don't worry, I'll handle it. You know me, I can fix anything … except Charlie's hair. I give. *(Races out upstage left dressing room door. Deedra takes a comb from dressing table, crosses to Charlie.)*
DEEDRA. Well, let's see what *I* can do with that mop of yours while Libby Ruth tries to work a miracle.
CHARLIE. I throw myself on the mercy of the court, your honor.
DEEDRA. *(During the following, she tries to style Charlie's hair, gives up, ditches the comb, gets a ribbon off dressing table, ties it in a bow on the brush handle.)* When Harris and I get ready for work in the morning, he asks why I bother curling my eyelashes and doing my hair. I tell him if I'm sending a perp away for twenty to life, I feel I should give the guy some eye candy to remember. It's a simple

act of charity. But that's who I am. I'm a giver.
CHARLIE. Last time we talked, you were looking for a splashy anniversary gift for Harris. You come up with anything?
DEEDRA. You bet! A brand, spankin' new *paralegal.* Marla was on my staff and I sent her over. I won't stand by and watch my husband work himself to death.
CHARLIE. That was actually very sweet.
DEEDRA. Sweet, hell! Until Harris has earned enough for us to retire to the South of France, I want that man *alive* and slaving away in that office! *(Excited, Libby Ruth runs in downstage left hallway door with an armload of items for Deedra's outfit.)*
LIBBY RUTH. Ooh, I do love a good challenge! Look, y'all! I found these great fabric remnants in Sedalia's workroom. Stand back! We are makin' some magic! *(Starts to work.)*
DEEDRA. Oh, God, how did we get into this?
CHARLIE. Senior Class Prom, no dates, halfway through a bottle of Chianti, the four of us swore we'd find our true loves and be each other's bridesmaids. If you hadn't picked the lock on your dad's liquor cabinet we wouldn't be in the predicament we're in today… totally your fault.
LIBBY RUTH. *(Drapes a beautiful piece of fabric, toga-style around Deedra, chirps.)* Ooh! I feel like one of those mice in *Cinderella!*
DEEDRA. Oh, that reminds me, Charlie. I have a man I want you to meet.
LIBBY RUTH. What reminded you of *that? (Ties scarf around Deedra's waist.)*
DEEDRA. He's an exterminator. *(To Charlie.) Very* successful. Owns his own company. His name is Fletcher and he—
CHARLIE. Let's stop right there. I am *not* going to meet this man, okay?
LIBBY RUTH. Because of his job? *(Drapes a length of fabric over Deedra's shoulders like a shawl.)*
CHARLIE. Because his name is *Fletcher!* I mean, *really,* can you think of a name that's less romantic? Kiss me, *Fletcher.* Hold me, *Fletcher.* Give me some of that hot monkey love, *Fletcher.* Nope. Not feeling it.
DEEDRA. You *can't* be serious!
CHARLIE. Serious as an Upper G.I.! A girl's gotta have standards. Mine may be low, but at least I've got 'em, baby. *(Libby Ruth fastens the shawl on one side with a silk flower corsage. The effect is surpris-*

ingly attractive.)
LIBBY RUTH. *(Admires her work.)* Well, looka here. I think I've gone and outdone myself this time. *(Sedalia sails in downstage left hallway door.)*
SEDALIA. Okay, girls, let's head 'em up and — *(Stares at Deedra. Then, to Libby Ruth.)* Now I see what you wanted with all those bits and pieces. Well … I believe you've done a fine job … considering what you had to work with.
LIBBY RUTH. *(To Deedra)* I'm almost certain she's referring to the *fabric*. *(Monette rushes in upstage right dressing room door, wears sparkly earrings and precariously high heels.)*
MONETTE. *(Eyes Deedra's costume, to Libby Ruth.)* So now she's wearing *that* in my wedding? *(To Deedra.)* What is it with you and Charlie today?!
DEEDRA. Oh, no, no, no. You lost your right — *for life* — to criticize what someone else is wearing after the stunt you pulled at our high school graduation.
MONETTE. Why do you always bring this up? *(To Sedalia.)* I didn't moon the crowd on purpose. It was a hundred and five in the shade, so all I wore under my graduation gown was antiperspirant.
LIBBY RUTH. Everyone was sitting in the bleachers on the football field, sweating buckets, and Monette didn't know that polyester gown had gotten stuck halfway up her back.
CHARLIE. And when she pranced across the stage to get her diploma … well, let's just say she showed a whole lot more than bad judgment. *(The three of them laugh. Sedalia scrutinizes Monette's skirt.)*
MONETTE. *(Catches Sedalia's inspection.)* Don't worry, I've learned my lesson. *(To the others.)* Okay, if that's all we've got for Deedra, fine. I guess everyone did the best they could. And anyway, *I'm* the main attraction of *this* rodeo. *(Models her outfit.)* So, how do I look? Gorgeous, right?
DEEDRA. And about a foot taller in those stilettos.
SEDALIA. *(Eyes Monette's cleavage.)* Trust me, darlin', every eye in the house will be riveted on you.
CHARLIE. If for no other reason than to see if you can actually keep those puppies stuffed inside that jacket.
MONETTE. Oh, you say that at all my weddings!
SEDALIA. Alright, then. It's show time, girls! *(Crosses to downstage left hallway door.)* I'll alert the troops and try to sober up the preacher! *(Exits. Monette runs to the upstage center chest, grabs cham-*

pagne bottle and flutes. Charlie finally gets brush out of her hair, tosses tissue box onto sofa.)
MONETTE. Okay, but we're having a little sippy before we go downstairs!
LIBBY RUTH. Here, Monette. Let me pour. *(Takes bottle, fills glasses.)* Isn't what we have flat-out wonderful? People are always telling me one of their deepest regrets is losing touch with old friends. But not us! We've kept our friendship alive ever since seventh grade. You know, I believe that makes us four in a million!
MONETTE. Well, I just want to say, having y'all in every one of my weddings means the world to me. Thank you for your love and support and for never letting jealousy about my looks get in the way of our friendship. And I really believe I've finally found the right man! Gavin Reed is the end of my rainbow! *(They cheer.)*
DEEDRA. *(Lifts her glass.)* To the happy couple! *(They toast.)*
CHARLIE. So, give us some details about this guy before we *finally* meet him at the altar. How long have you known him?
MONETTE. Almost two weeks. *(Takes a sip. The others freeze, exchange looks. Deedra knocks back her champagne, takes Libby Ruth's, knocks it back.)*
DEEDRA. *Two weeks?!* You yanked us out of our lives with no notice and had us drag ourselves back to what's left of our hometown so you can marry some guy you've known *two weeks?!* How do you know you even *like* him?
CHARLIE. Yeah, I've had the same brother *forty-six years* and the jury's still out on *that* one.
LIBBY RUTH. *(Rallies.)* Well, sometimes your heart knows if it's the real thing. And clearly you haven't seen the man bend over to pick up a set of keys. *(Fans herself at the memory.)*
MONETTE. *Thank* you, Libby Ruth! *(To Deedra.)* I am trying to have a wonderful, spontaneous romantic moment here! And hey, not everyone gets it right the first go 'round like you and Libby Ruth did.
DEEDRA. We're just worried for you. If this doesn't work, you'll be three for three! After that, the only men who'll give you a chance will be weirdos and knuckle-draggers like the ones who go for Charlie. *(Charlie shoots her a deadly look.)*
LIBBY RUTH. You can't write off the possibility of a whirlwind romance! Why shouldn't it work out?
CHARLIE. *Because* she hasn't known Gavin long enough. *(To*

Monette.) I bet you don't even know his middle name.
MONETTE. *(Clueless.)* Umm …
DEEDRA. I rest my case!
MONETTE. Can y'all just be happy for me?! I am getting married and I am getting married *now! (Sedalia sails in downstage left hallway door with a bridal bouquet and three nosegays.)*
SEDALIA. Okay, places, girls! *(Hands out the flowers.)* We're moving out!
DEEDRA. No, we are *not! (To Monette.)* You can't marry this guy!
MONETTE. Oh, yes I can!
CHARLIE. Sure you can, but you shouldn't!
LIBBY RUTH. She most certainly should!
SEDALIA. Oh, joy. Third time this month. Okay, ladies, there's only one way to settle this. *(Goes to downstage left table, takes a coin from a dish.)*
DEEDRA. You cannot be serious! You're not proposing we settle a life-altering decision by a flip of a—
SEDALIA. Call it! *(Flips the coin.)*
MONETTE. *(Immediately.)* Heads! *(Coin lands on the floor, all gather around, squint to see the coin. Beat. They squint again, bend lower. Beat.)*
DEEDRA. *(Stands.)* Oh, for heaven's sake. Who's got reading glasses?
LIBBY RUTH. Look on the dressing table, I'll check over here. *(As they scatter, each to find her glasses, Sedalia, unnoticed, quickly turns the coin "heads up." The others put on their glasses, race back to the coin, all bend over. Libby Ruth gets on her knees, peers at the coin.)* It's heads! *(Rises, she and Monette squeal, hug.)*
SEDALIA. Good, that's settled. *(Walks to downstage left hallway door, opens it.)* I'd like to remind you this wedding ceremony, in keeping with the high standards of Laurelton Oaks, will be conducted with grace and dignity. *(Cuts the niceties:)* Now, let's slam this turkey in the oven! Hit it! *(Exits.)*
MONETTE. Oh, I'm so happy! I truly believe this is going to work! Just trust me, please. *(Pointedly.)* And nobody better do *anything* to throw this ceremony off course, got it?! *(Then, happy.)* Come on, y'all! *(Exits downstage left hallway door.)*
DEEDRA. *(To the others.)* I just want to go on record as saying she's making a *gigantic mistake. (Exits downstage left hallway door.)*
CHARLIE. *(To Libby Ruth.)* If I blow my groceries or pass out

goin' down the aisle, just keep moving and leave me for dead. *(Sneezes repeatedly as she exits the downstage left hallway door. Libby Ruth floats to the sofa.)*
LIBBY RUTH. *(Elated.)* It's all so romantic … I give this sucker two months tops, but right now … *(Sighs happily, grabs tissue box.)* it's *so* romantic. Just puts a song in my heart. *(Sings loudly, off-key as she crosses to downstage left hallway door.)* AH, SWEET MYSTERY OF LIFE AT LAST I'VE FOUND YOU … *(Exits. Blackout.)*

Scene 2

A light comes up downstage right. Kari Ames-Bissette continues the speech to her wedding guests she began in Scene 1.

KARI. … Yes-sir-ee! I come from a long line of romantics. At my parents' twenty-fifth wedding anniversary, Daddy told the crowd his secret to a happy and successful marriage: "If you want to stay out of the doghouse, remember these three magic phrases — "It's my fault," "Let's eat out" and the sure-fire home run, "Honey, have you lost weight?" *(Giggles, to unseen "Todd.")* Words of wisdom, Todd! *(Laughs, sips champagne.)* Now, some of you may know I had a few … okay, a *lot* of rocky relationships over the years. And at one point I was so burned out on romance, I'd decided men were only good for two things: vehicle maintenance and grilling meat. And if I'd ever learned how to rotate my tires or flame kiss a T-bone, I might not be here today. *(Finishes a sip of champagne.)* Ooh, this is really tasty, isn't it? *(Her attention caught, to her "guests.")* Excuse me, y'all. *(Hollers, stern.)* Uncle Huell, I'm warning you, one foot closer to Aunt Viola and those cheese straws, you are gonna be in a world of pain, mister! … Anywho … *(Now a bit more relaxed, less nervous.)* But my mom and godmothers kept me from giving up on someday finding my true love … *(Starry-eyed.)* my *Todd* … and here we are! And I intend to always be there for them like they've been there for me — and each other. Although that notion was really put to the test a couple of years after Monette's last wedding. Boy howdy, *that* was a day to remember. A storm was

brewing, dark clouds were gathering … oh, and the weather was miserable, too … *(Cross fade, lights down on Kari. Sound effects: Thunder! Lightning! Lights up center stage on the upstairs sitting room at Laurelton Oaks. It's a summer afternoon, two years after Scene 1. The floral arrangements have changed, different throw pillows are on the sofa, a coffee table now sits downstage center in front of the sofa, two raincoats are piled on the downstage left side chair, trays of tiny sandwiches, bowls of pickles and other goodies are on upstage center chest, three corsage boxes are on downstage left table. Otherwise, the elegant room has remained the same. Monette enters downstage left hallway door in a skin-tight, ankle-length, gold lame bridesmaid dress, huge shoulder pads, long sleeves, skirt slit precariously high on one side, neckline plunges ridiculously low. Fans herself vigorously.)*
MONETTE. Hey, Charlie! I just figured out why they're called "hot flashes": because "scorching winds from the deserts of hell" takes too long to say. *(Looks around.)* Charlie? *(Spots closed upstage right dressing room door, crosses, knocks. Loud.)* Oh, come on now. You can't keep doing this, shug! Sure you're nervous, every bride gets the jitters on her big day! It's happens to me every single time *I* get married. What you need to do is hitch up those big girl panties and come on out of there. Don't you want to enjoy the joke you've pulled on us — making us wear all our old bridesmaid's dresses? Although this classic I picked for y'all to wear in mine has certainly stood the test of time better than others. *(Libby Ruth hurries in wearing a dowdy, unflattering floor-length bridesmaid's dress made of floral fabric, with a high neckline, short puffy sleeves, ruffles criss-cross the bodice down into a big sash around the waist that is tied in a huge bow in back, a matching large ruffle around the hem of the dress.)*
LIBBY RUTH. *(Happily.)* Well, the rain hasn't kept anyone away. Kari says the guest book is almost full.
MONETTE. *(Dry.)* Wow, you look like Little Spouse On The Prairie.
LIBBY RUTH. Yes, isn't it the sweetest thing you've ever seen? I still remember how big Preston's eyes got when he saw us all coming at him down that aisle. This is going to be such a beautiful — *(Looks around.)* Where's Charlie? She isn't—
MONETTE. Oh, yes she is.
LIBBY RUTH. She hasn't—
MONETTE. Oh, yes she has.

LIBBY RUTH. Oh, dear. *(Hurries to the door.)* Charlie, honey, it's time to get you ready to go downstairs. We need to get you hitched before the road floods and the only way out is the backstroke. And our corsages turned out so pretty; you'll just love them. Too bad they're not big enough to cover more of Monette's ta-tas.

MONETTE. Hey, better this than getting stuck in that nightmare from Deedra's wedding. *(Deedra enters in a long, straight lime green dress with a wide red waistband, white fake fur collar and cuffs with a short red capelet, the bottom edged with jingle bells. The dress was clearly made for a Christmas wedding. She carries a tote bag and a raincoat.*

LIBBY RUTH. *(In cahoots with Monette.)* So, Deedra, I guess you'll be taking off right after the ceremony?

MONETTE. Yeah, so she can hurry on up to Who-ville to steal Christmas! *(She and Libby Ruth collapse in a laughing fit.)*

DEEDRA. Cheap talk from Little Miss Cracker Barrel and A Streetwalker Named Desire.

LIBBY RUTH. I cannot believe Charlie saved these dresses all these years.

DEEDRA. In a twisted sort of way, I suppose we do deserve the humiliation of having to wear what we insisted *she* wear in our weddings.

MONETTE. Excuse me, but I think mine is still gorgeous. Turns out I've loved this bridesmaid's dress way longer than I ever loved that husband.

DEEDRA. *(Removes capelet, causing the bells to ring vigorously, studies it.)* Twenty-seven years ago a holiday wedding seemed like a good idea … then again, so did getting married. *(Libby Ruth and Monette exchange a concerned look. Sound effects: Thunder!)* Sorry I'm late; I had to paddle the last hundred miles.

LIBBY RUTH. We're so glad you're here. Our bride's locked in the dressing room with a bad case of cold feet. See if you can't talk some sense into her.

DEEDRA. Fine. *(Walks quickly to upstage right dressing room, pounds on the door.)* Okay, Charlie. The rest of us have tied the knot — some more than others — now it's your turn. So get your eco-friendly butt into that dress, suck it up and take your medicine like a woman.

MONETTE. Boy, if that sweet talk doesn't comfort her, nothing will.

LIBBY RUTH. *(Crosses to upstage right dressing room door, listens*

at the door. Then, low.) Do y'all think she's alright in there? *(They join her, lean in, ears to the door, behinds stuck out. Lights flicker, just as Sedalia, in another beautiful flowing caftan and signature ropes of pearls, hurries in downstage left hallway door fussing with a bridal bouquet, sees their behinds, stops in her tracks.)*
SEDALIA. Your timing's off, ladies. We wait 'til the *toast* for "bottoms up." *(The girls turn around. Re: their dresses.)* Ah! The "ugly bridesmaid's dress revenge." I haven't seen that in a while. One of my favorites.
LIBBY RUTH. Sedalia, there's a teensy problem. Charlie's a little anxious and—
SEDALIA. She's locked herself in the dressing room, of course. I can handle this. *(Knocks on the door.)* Miss Collins! This might be a good time to review that signed, notarized and paid-in-full contract of ours. In fact, let's focus on the phrase that helps me sleep at night: "non-refundable without exception." *(Presses her ear to the door, the others do the same.)* Charlie? Hello? *(Unseen, Charlie, in pale green, below-the-knee-length wedding dress and Birkenstocks, exits upstage left dressing room door, grabs a pickle from the tray, devours it, joins the others at the upstage right dressing room door.)*
MONETTE. Hmm. I still don't hear anything. Maybe we *should* be worried.
DEEDRA. Of course we should! If she's croaked and there's no ceremony, we'll have embarrassed ourselves in these ridiculous dresses for nothing! *(Beat.)*
CHARLIE. *(Whispers anxiously.)* What's going on?
MONETTE. *(Whispers.)* Charlie's locked herself in again and if you have any — *(Realizes.)* Charlie! *(Everyone turns to her.)* Where did you come from?
CHARLIE. The other dressing room. *(Indicates upstage left dressing room. Libby Ruth turns the knob on upstage right dressing room door, it opens. She and Monette slump.)* I just had to lie down a minute, close my eyes and think.
SEDALIA. Good idea! And *now* you should think about slipping those un-pedicured piggies of yours into a nice pair of shoes a grown-up bride-to-be might wear. We don't want to frighten our guests, do we? *(Lights flicker. To the others.)* Not to worry, we're fully prepared for a candlelight ceremony in the event of a power failure. Now, the guests are all seated and waiting for the main event. So, chop, chop, ladies! *(Hands bridal bouquet to Charlie.)*

CHARLIE. *(As Sedalia exits downstage left hallway door.)* We'll be ready! Thanks for everything, Ms. Ellicott! We'll be right down and — *(Then, conspiratorially, to the others.)* Good, she's gone! Here's what we're going to do. *(To Libby Ruth.)* You bring the car around to the back door. *(To Deedra and Monette.)* You two create a diversion, maybe start a small fire in the ladies' room downstairs. Yeah, that's good! I'll slip out and no one will notice. Everyone in?
LIBBY RUTH. *(Laughs nervously.)* Oh, Charlie, you cut-up. On your tenth anniversary, you and Fletcher will have such a good laugh about this. *(Low to Monette and Deedra as Charlie crosses to downstage left hallway door, opens it, checks the hallway.)* We could be in trouble, girls. Follow my lead. *(Goes to Charlie, brings her center stage above sofa. Then, sweetly, to Charlie.)* Shug, I think now might be the time for you to tell us exactly what's going on in that head of yours. The three of us have looked forward to this day for years —
DEEDRA. A day we never, ever, ever, *ever* thought would happen. Ever.
LIBBY RUTH. *(Shoots Deedra a look. To Charlie.)* And we want to make it the happiest day of your life, but we're sensing some conflicting emotions here. Whatever it is, just get it off your chest. You know you can say anything to us.
CHARLIE. *(Deep breath.)* Okay. *(Exhales.)* The truth is, after years of watching everybody else march down the aisle, I think I may have gotten carried away with the whole idea of finally getting *my* shot at it. The gifts, the wedding showers, friends having to pay off bets when they heard I was finally getting married.
MONETTE. *(Primps in the mirror, to herself.)* Yeah, that was a fifty buck ding I never saw coming. *(The others stare at her, she notices.)* What?
CHARLIE. I'm not exactly a hundred percent convinced I'm ready for this. And I'm never at my best when I'm forced to wear a dress. But I think it's just now starting to sink in how much everything's going to change once I've said "I do." I don't *want* to make room for his clothes in my closet. I've had it to myself all these years, it's *mine!* And I mean *really* … is the grand achievement of my life going to be *marrying an exterminator?!*
MONETTE. But you do *love* Fletcher, don't you?
CHARLIE. Of course. He's sweet, loves the outdoors and hates to shave. We have a lot in common. But there *are* issues. One is, his mother hates me. She thinks I tried to poison her when I took

her tofu enchiladas for Sunday supper. And the rest of his relatives wouldn't know good nutrition if it bit 'em in the butt. I mean, can I really marry into a family that thinks *gravy* is a beverage?

DEEDRA. This is just now registering? For heaven's sake, you've gone out with Fletcher for nearly two years!

CHARLIE. Yeah, but do I really want him living in my house, touching my things, asking me where I'm going? Complaining every time I go out on a date?

LIBBY RUTH. You know, there may be some gray areas in the concept of *marriage* we need to clear up for you. Charlie, love is a precious gift that makes life richer, fuller. At the very end, when your friends are gazing down at you in your casket, don't you want them to say, "Charlie really filled her life with love."

CHARLIE. Hell, no! I want them to point and scream, *"Look! She's moving!"*

MONETTE. Why didn't I realize this before? Charlie, you have stage fright! It happens all the time with performers at my club, particularly on amateur night. And I know exactly how to fix it, but unfortunately we don't have a fifth of Wild Turkey and a funnel handy. Oh, shoot. I'll improvise. *(Grabs Charlie, quickly bends her over the couch, pats her back rhythmically.)* Got to get some blood and oxygen into the old brain pan. That'll get rid of the fog and confusion.

LIBBY RUTH. *(Jumps on it.)* And you know what? This will be the perfect time for us to do what my sister, Viola, calls a "Marriage Go 'Round" where the women get to remind the bride of all the good things about married life.

DEEDRA. *(Dry.)* Me first: tax deductions. I'm done.

LIBBY RUTH. *(Shoots Deedra a stern look. Then.)* Here's a good one about how rewarding *compromise* can be in a marriage. Now, I couldn't love Preston more even if he was dipped in chocolate. But one time we hit a speed bump. See, I wanted him to get away from our diner more often and take ballroom dance classes with me. Well, he agreed, but only if I'd go with him to monster truck pulls. Well, I hated the thought, but I *had* to give in. And the darned thing is, I really got to liking them — *(Gets into it, lusty.)* those *huge, powerful, throbbing* machines! *(Composes herself. Then, pointedly.)* So, see? Compromise can be *very* rewarding.

MONETTE. Well, I say, keep on truckin', hot mama! And you are absolutely right. Marriage *can* be fun most of the time.

DEEDRA. Yeah, but the trouble is, you're married *all* of the time. *(Charlie raises up, a confused look on her face.)*
LIBBY RUTH. *(Quickly pushes Charlie over the back of the sofa. Then low, pointedly.)* Deedra, you aren't really helping, hon. I'm thinking you don't understand the goal we're shootin' for here.
MONETTE. *(As she continues to pat Charlie's back.)* Yeah, Deedra! The last train to love and fulfillment is pulling out of the station and if we don't get this forty-nine-year-old spinster on board, she can kiss any shot at happiness good-bye forever! *(Charlie looks up. Monette covers.)* And you know I say that in the most encouraging way possible.
CHARLIE. Any more encouragement like that, I'm hanging myself in the toilet.
LIBBY RUTH. *(Pointedly.)* And now I believe Deedra's got something extra-positive and sweet she's wanting to say about marriage. Alright, make it nice.
DEEDRA. *(Explodes.)* For the love of Mike! Let's just get on with it! Throw your cards on the table, Charlie. Are you going to leave that poor bug zapper at the altar or go ahead and marry him and ruin your life anyway? *(Sound effects: Thunder! Lightning!)*
LIBBY RUTH. *(Takes Deedra's hand, leads her to upstage left dressing room door.)* You know, Deedra, I just remembered something you need to take a look at. You'll really like it. It's just inside that door.
DEEDRA. Where? I don't see any—
LIBBY RUTH. *(Shoves Deedra into the dressing room, closes the door, holds onto the door knob. Then, calm, turns back to Charlie.)* Anyway, Monette's right. Married life can be a lot of fun, if you approach it like the adventure it is. *(Struggles to keep Deedra from opening the door.)*
CHARLIE. *(Raises up.)* Look, you three have always had someone to go with you through life's ups and downs and I thought I wanted that, too. Maybe I still do ... I don't know ... Maybe I don't ... Good lord, what is wrong with me?!
MONETTE. Honey, you sure this doesn't boil down to having nerves about the honeymoon? 'Cause it's not like Fletcher's never seen you in your birthday suit. Enjoy yourselves, have fun, try new things, go wild! But speaking from personal experience, never do *anything* you'd be embarrassed to explain to the paramedics.
CHARLIE. Well ... maybe it is just last-minute nerves. I mean, I've come this far and everyone's waiting. *(Determined.)* No! This is

the right thing to do ... I think ... isn't it?
DEEDRA. *(Calls from offstage.)* Let me out of here this minute!
LIBBY RUTH. *(Loud, through the door.)* The knob's stuck, sweetheart. Give me a sec! *(Back to Charlie.)* Of course it's the right thing to do. You see, Charlie, you get a little oxygen flowing, you're making good decisions, you've got clarity of mind. Honey, we're your best friends, we'd never steer you wrong. *(Then, brightly.)* Now, go slap on a little blush ... maybe a *whole lot,* pretty yourself up and get ready to be the star of the show! *(Charlie stares at the dress.)*
CHARLIE. Why on earth doesn't somebody make wedding *pants?!* *(Exits the upstage right dressing room door.)*
LIBBY RUTH. *(Calls, happily supportive.)* And just think Charlie, you're going downstairs into the arms of the one and only man you'll have sex with for the rest of your life! *(Louder.)* The *rest of your life!*
MONETTE. Shug, I'm not so sure that was the deal-closer we were looking for. *(Sound effects: Thunder! Lightning! Deedra yanks open upstage left dressing room.)*
DEEDRA. *(Steamed.)* What, exactly, do you think you're doing?!
LIBBY RUTH. Well, I'm sorry, Deedra, but we were teetering on the brink of disaster and your negative attitude isn't helping.
MONETTE. *(Gasps.)* That's exactly what Gavin said to *me* this morning! Y'all don't mind if I bring the conversation back to myself right quick, do you?
DEEDRA. We never do.
MONETTE. Okay, the first two years of this marriage have been great, but ... *(With difficulty.)* I think Gavin's losing interest in me. See, he's developed this obsession with baking and started taking night classes at a culinary academy. It's all he thinks about! It's like Gavin would rather squeeze a pastry bag than *me!*
LIBBY RUTH. Oh, Monette, you're just making a mountain out of a molehill.
MONETTE. And I'm the one getting to be the size of a mountain! I'm scarfing down cream puffs, napoleons and éclairs by the bushel, just to be supportive. But I swear, the way I'm blowing up, a little helium, some rope and they can float *me* in the Macy's Thanksgiving Parade. *(Then.)* Y'all, I think it's going to cost me my man.
LIBBY RUTH. You always do this, sugar! Now, you're beautiful and you've finally got a happy marriage. It's not like Gavin's carrying on with other women.

MONETTE. Oh, yes he is! Martha Stewart, Betty Crocker, all of 'em! Gavin only thinks about cooking. Last week I said, "I bet you don't even remember what my favorite flower is, do you?" He said, "Sure, I do. Pillsbury Self-Rising, right?"
DEEDRA. I say take what you can get, Monette. At least your new car smell lasted this long.
LIBBY RUTH. Alright, that's it! Deedra, you haven't poked your head out of that black cloud since you got here. What is wrong?
DEEDRA. It's nothing.
MONETTE. The heck it isn't! Spill it, sister. You're bringing us all down. Let's talk it out and get it done!
DEEDRA. I'm telling you, this is not the time to discuss it. *(Unseen by the others, Charlie reenters from upstage right dressing room, now in a pair of heels.)*
LIBBY RUTH. Of course it is! Tell us now! Come on!
DEEDRA. *(Explodes.)* Fine! Harris left me! He's filed for divorce! *(The others are dumbstruck. Beat.)*
LIBBY RUTH. Oh, sweetheart! *(Hugs her.)*
MONETTE. Dear God! *(Puts her arm around Deedra.)* Dee-Dee, precious, why didn't you tell us before now?
CHARLIE. *(Panicked.)* No, no, no, *no!* *(Wobbles on her high heels, paces, mini meltdown.)* This can't be happening! Deedra, you and Libby Ruth had the only marriages that ever worked. I can't breathe! I need air! *(Sound effects: Thunder!)* Wait! I know what this is! I'm having a *smart attack*. This wedding is a big mistake! No way I'm marrying the bug zapper now! *(Races through upstage right dressing room door, slams, locks it.)*
DEEDRA. And *that's* why I didn't tell you before now.
LIBBY RUTH. But you and Harris have been together almost thirty years! This is terrible!
DEEDRA. *(Sighs.)* Harris left me weeks ago and I've been trying to deal with it. I convinced myself I could get through today because I didn't want to be the one to break our promise and not be here for the wedding. And I've been nothing but a wet blanket. I'm sorry for the way I've been acting. This is supposed to be Charlie's big day. Get her out of there, Libby Ruth. She'll listen to you. *(Libby Ruth hurries to upstage right dressing room door, tries the knob.)*
LIBBY RUTH. Unlock the door, Charlie! Just because Deedra's marriage has gone down the crapper doesn't mean yours will, too!

(Grabs a nail file off the makeup table, tries to pick the lock.)
MONETTE. *(To Deedra.)* I know I should mind my own business, but at this moment, it's not half as interesting as yours. So, how about you give us the facts, fast and dirty? Then, after we've dragged Charlie to the altar, we will track down Harris and kill him like the cur dog he is.
DEEDRA. *(Sincere.)* What a sweet thing to say. *(Then:)* Okay, remember *Marla,* the paralegal *I* sent over to help him when he was swamped? Well, she helped him out, alright — out of his trousers, out of our house and out of our marriage! *(Walks to upstage center chest to the trays of food.)* See, I found out they'd been carrying on for over a year! These last few weeks I've been a wreck. But I'm not sad anymore. Now I just want *revenge! (Bites a pickle in half. The others share a look of surprise.)*
LIBBY RUTH. And while you get it, be sure to take him for every nickel he's got! *(Off their surprise.)* Hey, I may be a romantic, but I'm not an idiot. Okay, I'm going down to tell Sedalia what's happened. I'll ask her to open the bar *now,* keep the guests distracted and delay the ceremony 'til Charlie calms down. *(Races out downstage left hallway door.)*
MONETTE. *(Calls after her.)* Yeah, good plan! An open bar can fix *anything*! *(Off Deedra's look.)* Hey, whoever said laughter is the best medicine clearly never had a margarita.
DEEDRA. I never thought I'd find myself in this predicament.
MONETTE. Girlfriend, don't you worry; Harris and his little nymphet are going to get their just desserts. Take my word for it, when a woman steals your husband, there's no better revenge than to let her *keep* him.
DEEDRA. I wonder when it will dawn on the two of them that they're trying to screw over a *judge.* I know every legal pit bull in D.C. I just retained Jamison Moyers, Esquire, himself. That shark and I are going to clean house!
MONETTE. Now *that* sounds like the Honorable Deedra Wingate we know and love. *(Gives Deedra a hug. Libby Ruth races in downstage left hallway door.)*
LIBBY RUTH. Sedalia's on her way. She says she's always prepared for this kind of situation and has a sure-fire way to get Charlie out of the dressing room!
MONETTE. Thank goodness! If anyone can persuade her, she — *(Sedalia charges in downstage left hallway door, wielding a massive axe.)*

SEDALIA. Stand back ladies! I'm getting this bride to the altar!
DEEDRA. You can't be serious!
SEDALIA. Oh, but I am. I've built a good deal of my reputation in the events industry on the fact that we've never lost a bride here at Laurelton Oaks. And we never will — at least not on *my* watch.
MONETTE. You'd actually hack through that door?
SEDALIA. You bet your sweet patoot! My reputation is worth a lot more to me than this chunk of wood. *(Hoists the axe, ready to bash down the door. Just then, Charlie opens the door.)*
CHARLIE. Alright, I've thought it over and — *(Sees Sedalia, screams! Libby Ruth, Monette and Deedra scream! Sedalia lowers the axe.)* What are you doing?!
SEDALIA. *(Unruffled.)* My job. Now, the Wedding March will start in exactly two minutes and I expect you — *all* of you — on that landing the moment the first note is played. And ladies, if any of you put another hitch in the proceedings … *(Picks up the axe, then, pointedly.)* remember, I'm a *master problem solver. (Then, brightly.)* Alright, girls, put some hustle in your bustle! *(Exits downstage left hallway door.)*
MONETTE. Now, there's a woman who knows how to get 'er done. If she ever runs for public office, she's got my vote!
CHARLIE. Geez, *that* little encouraging nudge certainly cleared things up. *(Deep breath.)* Don't worry, I know what I have to do now.
LIBBY RUTH. See, love really *does* conquer all. And I know that deep down inside, *in a place that may be hard for her to reach right now,* Deedra wants to tell you to absolutely take a chance on love and never, ever postpone joy. *(Pinches Deedra.)* Don't you, Deedra?
CHARLIE. No, you've all said enough. I'm through acting the fool and I really do appreciate your helping me through this crisis. I'll just go in there and finish up. *(Exits upstage right dressing room door. The others breathe an audible sigh of relief.)*
LIBBY RUTH. Whew! We barely pulled *that* off. Okay, let's move it before Sedalia comes back with a S.W.A.T. team! *(Grabs corsages, hurriedly pins one on Monette as she quickly checks her makeup in the dressing table mirror. On the sofa, Deedra pulls a pair of heels from her bag, slips into them.)*
MONETTE. Fletcher owes us big time for this. He's killing my bugs free *for life! (Unseen behind them, Charlie, in a raincoat, baseball cap, clutches her purse, tiptoes toward downstage left hallway*

door.) But I really think sharing *my* experience turned the tide for Charlie. She's — *(Sees Charlie in the mirror.)* She's making a break for it!

LIBBY RUTH. Stop her! *(Libby Ruth and Monette go for Charlie who dodges them and sprints to the other side of the sofa in close proximity to Deedra and downstage left hallway door.)*

CHARLIE. *(Wild-eyed.)* Don't come near me! I've made up my mind and I'm not doing this! This is one big, fat mistake I refuse to make!

LIBBY RUTH. Deedra, help us! She's got to do the right thing! Say something!

DEEDRA. You're right. *(Beat.)* Run, Charlie, run! *(Charlie races out downstage left hallway door.)* Get away before it's too late! Go! Go! *(Libby Ruth and Monette run to the door, Deedra grabs them, holds them back. They wrestle, Libby Ruth and Monette finally wrench themselves out of Deedra's grip.)*

MONETTE. *(To Deedra.)* Why did you say that?

DEEDRA. Look, I tried to be a team player but Charlie obviously knows what she wants and it's not this.

LIBBY RUTH. Oh, for heaven's sake! *(Grabs her raincoat off downstage left side chair puts it on, calls out the downstage left hallway door.)* Runaway bride! Runaway bride! *(To the others.)* And if that's not bad enough, she'll get mud on that dress and never be able to consign it! *(Races out downstage left hallway door. Monette runs to the downstage "window" facing the audience. Peers out.)*

MONETTE. Libby Ruth better hurry, Charlie just rammed her way out the door! Good Lord! She just did a perfect broad jump over the koi pond!

DEEDRA. *(Runs to the window, looks out.)* There goes a woman who *absolutely* does not want to tie the knot.

MONETTE. Ooh! Libby Ruth's gaining on her.

DEEDRA. Don't count Sedalia out. Even with that axe, she's making good time!

MONETTE. Come on! *(Grabs Deedra's hand, pulls her toward downstage left hallway door. Scoops up their raincoats.)*

DEEDRA. What are we doing?!

MONETTE. Being supportive and joining the winning team! Now that Charlie's said "I *don't,*" we're going to hotwire the groom's truck, the one with the giant dead roach on top, grab Libby Ruth and Charlie and hightail it out of the county. If this thing's going to

hell in a handcart, let's hop in and enjoy the ride! What do you say?
DEEDRA. I say … that's what friends are for!
MONETTE. Yeah, mama! Woo-hoo!! *(They slap high fives, race out the downstage left hallway door. Sound effects: Thunder! Lightning!) Blackout.)*

End of Act One

ACT TWO

Scene 1

A light comes up downstage right. Kari Ames-Bissette continues the speech to her wedding guests she began in Act One, Scene 1. She is slightly more relaxed than before, a bit tipsy — not drunk — from her single flute of champagne.

KARI. *(Sips, big smile, re: champagne.)* Wow! This is *spectacular!* But it's gone straight to my head. I'd better watch it before I say something inappropriate ... like a woman walks into a bar, says, "I just got an exercise bike for my husband." Her friend says, "Hey, great trade!" *(Laughs, stops short. To Todd.)* Don't worry, honey. Just a little bridal speech humor. You're a keeper. *(Gives him thumbs up.)* This place is special to me because some of my godmothers were married here and because in this very room my life took a radical shift. You know, happiness really *can* take you by surprise; you just have to be brave enough to embrace it. *(Sips.)* And a couple of slugs of *this* could sure ratchet up your courage. *(Her attention caught.)* Here we go again. *(Louder.)* Aunt Viola, you get down off that chair and stop throwing butter mints at Uncle Huell! You're just egging him on! *(Then:)* Now, where was I? Oh, yes. About a year ago, I was here for a wedding and, oh boy, was *that* ever one for the books! *Wild* doesn't even begin to describe that evening! I found out throwing the perfect, elegant wedding is like hang-gliding, synchronized swimming or teaching a ferret to fetch. It looks *really* easy ... until you try it ... *(Laughs happily, sips. Cross fade, lights down on Kari. Lights up center stage on upstairs sitting room at Laurelton Oaks. It's an autumn evening, four years after Charlie fled the altar. The floral arrangements have changed, different pillows are on the sofa, champagne in a bucket, flutes and snacks in bowls are on upstage center chest. A new chair is downstage left, a painting is now on the wall over the table next to it. Deedra, in an elegant, floor-length gown, a corsage of orchids on one shoulder, talks on her phone as she*

hurries in from upstage left dressing room, crosses downstage right to dressing table, checks her makeup in the mirror, then nervously paces.)
DEEDRA. ... Oh, you'll be missed, Barbara, but Jamison and I understand you can't just leave the campaign trail. And of course you've got our vote! I've always believed politicians and diapers should be changed regularly. And for the same reason. *(Laughs.)* ... Yes, we did decide to honeymoon in Paris, so the whole wedding is French-themed — the food, the wine. And the bridesmaids and I are all wearing elegant French gowns and we'll — *(Libby Ruth enters the downstage left hallway door, in the costume of a Moulin Rouge can-can girl — taffeta dress with spaghetti straps on a frilly bodice, ankle-length skirt cut high in center front, multiple-multi-colored can cans underneath skirt, mid-calf, black pumps, feathers in her hair. She carries a small, stuffed toy poodle which she sets on the sofa.)*
LIBBY RUTH. Can we throw a wedding? Yes we *can-can!* *(Twirls around, tosses up the back of her skirt, squeals.)* Whee!
DEEDRA. *(Into phone.)* Gotta go, Barbara. Une petite problem-o just pranced through the door! *(Hangs up.)* What *is* that you're wearing?!
LIBBY RUTH. Surprise! It's my wedding gift to you. You told me I could pick out the bridesmaids' outfits as long as they were French and very stylish! So, voila!
DEEDRA. I meant French and stylish as in elegant gowns like mine!
LIBBY RUTH. You never said anything about elegant gowns. You said you wanted this wedding to be fun and festive, a real party! And what's more fun and festive than a *costume* party? *(Picks up poodle, baby talks.)* Isn't that right, Pierre?
DEEDRA. Oh, no, no, no! Swear to me you didn't let Charlie and Monette loose in a costume shop! Knowing them, they'll show up in — *(Just then, Charlie bursts through the downstage left hallway door in a sexy French maid's outfit: short black taffeta skirt held up by frilly white petticoats, tiny, ruffled white apron tied in a big bow in back, very low-cut top, lacy white cap on her head, black pumps with big black bows, carries a feather duster.)*
CHARLIE. *(Clearly uncomfortable.)* I feel like a French-fried freak in this.
DEEDRA. Oh — mon — Dieu! *(Plops on the sofa, her head in her hand.)*
CHARLIE. I mean, this is ridiculous! How could a maid clean a

toilet in this get-up? You lean over … *(Demonstrates, her behind to the audience.)* you flash the boss your *particulars,* there goes your job. Totally illogical.
DEEDRA. *(Frustrated.)* This is unbelievable! *(Re: Charlie.)* And in a million years I wouldn't have thought anyone could've gotten the *Countess of Compost* into an outfit like *that!* What did it take, a bet, a bribe, blackmail?
LIBBY RUTH. You know, I tried all those, but no luck. So I took her to brunch.
CHARLIE. Yeah, behind that sweet, innocent face is a scheming manipulator. She knows you get a couple of Bloody Marys in me, I'll agree to anything. And there's a long line of no-count guys who'd back me up on that statement.
LIBBY RUTH. Oh, stop! You look adorable. *(Baby talk to toy poodle.)* Doesn't she, Pierre? Yes, she does.
CHARLIE. Okay, fine. But I can't wait to get out of this little number!
LIBBY RUTH. *(Naughty.)* I can't wait to get out of mine, either. Preston went absolutely *wild* when he saw me in this. In fact, he liked it so much, I almost didn't get out the door. Looks like your wedding might benefit us all!
DEEDRA. Always happy to help. *(Then, to Charlie.)* Wait! You didn't let Sedalia see you come in, did you?
CHARLIE. After she *banished* me from here *forever?* Contrary to how I look at the moment, my mama didn't raise no fool; I've seen how Sedalia handles an axe.
DEEDRA. Well, there's *one* advantage to the costume concept. Your outfit might throw her off the scent long enough for us to get through the "I do's."
CHARLIE. I just wish Sedalia would let it go. It's been, what, four years now? Heck, even *Fletcher's* forgiven me for running out on him. And we'd probably be friends if his mom would stop leaving me the occasional reminder of how much she hates me.
LIBBY RUTH. How occasional?
CHARLIE. I'm down to four bags of flaming dog poo on my porch a week. And I'm starting to wonder: what *is* that woman feeding her chihuahua?
DEEDRA. Okay, okay, this misunderstanding about what I wanted all of you to wear is my fault. I should've spelled it out, and I do know your heart was in the right place, Libby Ruth. But what I

don't know is what to do to fix it.
LIBBY RUTH. Hold on. There's no problem. You're gorgeous, Deedra, like somethin' out of those fashion magazines with half-naked, hungry-lookin' girls on the covers. *(Baby talk to dog.)* Isn't she gorgeous, Pierre? Yes, she is!
CHARLIE. Yeah, come on, Deedra. You said you want tonight to be special and trust me, it is, because it's the *only* time you'll *ever* catch me dressed like this in public. I say let's roll with it.
DEEDRA. Well … *(Gives in.)* Oh, why not?! At least this wedding will be memorable. Besides, I'd say you two have pushed this French theme about as far over the top as it can go. *(Just then, Monette sails through downstage left hallway door in full Marie Antoinette costume: a lacy floor-length dress decorated with bows, ribbons, ruffles, very low-cut at the neck, three-quarter length lace-edged sleeves, skirt padded wide on either side. She wears a tall powdered white wig, ostrich plumes worked into the top, carries a lace fan and a tiny, drawstring purse/reticule. Deedra gasps. Libby Ruth and Charlie are delighted.)*
MONETTE. Hello, rabble!
DEEDRA. And I'm *wrong* again!
LIBBY RUTH. Wow! That dress suits you to a "T," Monette.
MONETTE. *(Grandly.)* That's Monette *Antoinette* to you, peasants!
CHARLIE. Accept it, Deedra. You're stuck with three French tarts. *(Monette bustles to the dressing table, admires herself in the mirror.)*
MONETTE. Ooh, tonight's going to be fabulous! Everything's *so* pretty downstairs and most of us look terrific! Shoot, you could have cataracts in both eyes on a real foggy night, and even *Charlie* might pass for sexy.
CHARLIE. Why is there never a guillotine handy when you really need one?
LIBBY RUTH. Speaking of painful separations, how did Harris handle it when you told him you're marrying your divorce lawyer?
DEEDRA. Not well. Since he'd dumped Marla, he'd been knocking himself out trying to win me back these last few years. I'll admit it was touching in a way. He really seemed like the old Harris … only with a whole lot less money. Jamison really outdid himself with the settlement.
MONETTE. So, you were getting your jollies making Harris work to win you back *and* dating Jamison *at the same time?* Color me impressed! *(Plops on the couch, fights with her skirt.)*
LIBBY RUTH. Why, Your Honor, I had no idea you could be

such a little vixen. *(Baby talk to toy poodle.)* We sure didn't, did we, Pierre? *(Deedra grabs poodle.)*
DEEDRA. Okay, nap time for Pierre. *(Baby talk to dog.)* You're creeping me out. Yes, you are! *(Tosses it behind the sofa.)* To be honest, there was a time I actually thought I *might* take Harris back. I've been very torn. But I love Jamison and I'm going to marry him. Tonight! *(They all cheer, delighted.)*
LIBBY RUTH. It's so beautiful that you've opened up your heart to love again. At this stage in life, it's really a brave and wonderful thing for you to do.
CHARLIE. Yeah, yeah. Rub it in. Two men for Deedra, three for Monette, one sex-crazed fry cook for the can-can girl and zip-a-roonie for me.
MONETTE. Excuse me, but you've had your chances. And now men may not be interested in you because they sense your deeply-ingrained need for revenge that can surface out of nowhere.
DEEDRA. Okay, let's get this fixed: court's in session. Monette, you've been sniping at Charlie ever since you waltzed into the room. What's going on?
CHARLIE. Gavin's mad at her and she's blaming me. I swear I didn't do anything malicious. I simply called Monette last Tuesday and left a message wishing her a happy fifty-third birthday and —
MONETTE. And that's all you two need to know about that.
CHARLIE. Monette made me vow I'd never speak of it. *(Beat.)* But she didn't say I couldn't *show* you! *(Grabs Monette's little purse/reticule. Monette screams, jumps up, chases Charlie around sofa. Charlie calls.)* Libby Ruth, here! *(Tosses the purse to her.)* Check her driver's license!
MONETTE. No! *(Lunges for Libby Ruth who tosses the purse to Deedra who rummages inside, pulls out a driver's license, holds it at arm's length, studies it.)*
DEEDRA. They've got your date of birth wrong! *Really* wrong.
MONETTE. *(Guiltily.)* Okay, look. I threw a big fundraiser at my club for a Congressman and he owed me a favor. And he had a friend at the D.M.V. and —
LIBBY RUTH. So you and Gavin had a little fight because you lied on your driver's license about your age?
MONETTE. No! We had a *terrible* fight because he *found out* — thanks to Charlie! — that I have lied to *him* about my age all these years.

DEEDRA. Incredible! Do you stay awake nights *looking* for ways to sabotage your marriage? How did you pull off something like that?
MONETTE. Well, when we first met, I really liked him but was afraid he preferred younger women, so … I got my license fixed and … Gavin has always believed I'm younger than I really am. *(Beat.)* Seven years younger. *(The others exchange an incredulous look, then burst out laughing. Then, pouty:)* What?! Well, I *could* be. I take really good care of my skin. *(More laughter.)* Fine. But just see if any of you get an invitation to my fiftieth birthday party *four years from now!*
LIBBY RUTH. But Gavin knows we all graduated high school the same year. *That* didn't bring up any questions?
MONETTE. I simply told him I was a child genius and they accelerated me seven grades in school. *(The others are open-mouthed with surprise.)* Gavin's always been impressed I have friends who are so much *older*. I told him I look on it as a type of Senior Outreach.
DEEDRA. What?! *(Fumes.)* Oh, I'll show you some Senior Outreach! *(Lunges for Monette, Libby Ruth and Charlie hold her back.)*
MONETTE. I can't understand why Gavin's making such a big deal of this. Y'all know I don't ask much from a relationship. I just want a man to accept me for who I pretend to be.
CHARLIE. That is so like you, Monette. Always thinking you can get by with breaking rules and doing just what you — *(Just then, Sedalia calls from offstage.)*
SEDALIA. Hey, ladies! Are you decent?
CHARLIE. I'm a dead woman! Hide me! *(Drops to the floor behind Monette's wide skirt. Sedalia bursts into the room wearing a black beret and red scarf tied at her neck and a black caftan, carries a tray of macaroons.)*
SEDALIA. *(Exuberant.)* Ooh-la-la, y'all! Let's par-tay on zee Champs Elysee! *(Plops tray on the upstage center chest.)* Girls, I cannot tell you how refreshing this French theme and costume idea is! I couldn't resist joining in.
DEEDRA. At this point, the more the merrier. Vive le France!
SEDALIA. I am so tired of off-the-shoulder, cookie cutter bridesmaids dresses. *This* is a fresh new take and I love it! Très magnifique! Now, I've got to run downstairs. Oh, and Libby Ruth, Kari did a great job helping with the table arrangements. That girl's a pistol. Unfortunately, when my nephew came over to lend her a hand,

they ended up in a big, ugly argument about women's rights.
LIBBY RUTH. *(Clearly rattled by this information.)* Oh, no. I'm sorry. I hope it didn't get too uncomfortable.
SEDALIA. I pulled Kari aside and explained that women will never be equal to men … until they can walk down the street with a bald head and a beer gut and still think they're sexy. *(Then.)* At least I got her to laugh and calm down. Since then the two of them have cut each other a wide berth. *(Crosses to downstage left hallway door.)* And speaking of which, I thank all of you for respecting my request that your friend, Charlie, not be here this evening. I know it was hard leaving her out, but I appreciate your understanding my position. *(Checks her watch. Brightly.)* Alright, we've started the countdown, mon petites fromages.
MONETTE. Wait. Did you just call us your little cheeses?
SEDALIA. Probably. My French stinks but I'm wild for brie. Au revoir! *(Exits. Charlie stands.)*
CHARLIE. That was close. Man, I am *so* on Old Eagle Eye's radar. *(To Monette.)* I have to say, I'm surprised you didn't rat me out.
MONETTE. Oh, I thought about it. But if I get even a *little* blood on this costume, the rental place will keep my deposit.
DEEDRA. You know I appreciate your willingness to sneak back in here today, Charlie. I really do love this old house and, besides, getting married in Laurelton keeps it far enough away from D.C. that Harris won't feel like I'm rubbing his nose in it. Once the music starts, just keep your head down and make a beeline for the minister. Sedalia's not about to make a scene.
CHARLIE. You're really that confident I can get away with this?
DEEDRA. Not at all. But one of my greatest strengths is I'm excellent at giving advice that I would *never* follow.
LIBBY RUTH. *(Rallies, then brightly.)* Okay girls, before we put this soufflé in the oven, let's make sure our bride's all ready. *(Monette and Charlie hurry to the upstage center chest, pours champagne into flutes.)* I think we have some questions for her, *don't we, girls?*
DEEDRA. You're not serious! Aren't we a bit long in the tooth for this game?
CHARLIE. Sure we are, but, hey, we're too long in the tooth to be *bridesmaids* and we're still doing *that!* So, go with it! It's tradition! *(Helps Monette pass out the champagne.)*
MONETTE. Okay. I'll start. There are four treasures you must have before you go to the altar. So … tell us what you have that's

something old.
DEEDRA. *(Gives in.)* Easy. That would be *me!*
CHARLIE. Au contraire. You're not the one who aged *seven years overnight.*
DEEDRA. That's right! Monette, you're my *something old. (Laughter.)* Sip! *(They sip.)*
LIBBY RUTH. Now, tell us what you have that's *something new.*
DEEDRA. *(Delight.)* A sex life! *(They cheer.)* Sip! *(They sip.)*
MONETTE. And what do you have that's *something borrowed?*
DEEDRA. The money to throw this wedding! *(They cheer.)* Sip! *(They sip.)*
CHARLIE. Now tell us what you have that's *something blue.*
DEEDRA. Um … do varicose veins count?
LIBBY RUTH. I forgot! Kari's got a blue garter for you, Deedra. I'll run get it.
MONETTE. No, let *me.* I want to peek at the crowd and see if Gavin got over himself and decided to show up.
LIBBY RUTH. But go down the back stairs so no one sees you.
MONETTE. I don't care if they do. And if anyone has a problem with the costume I chose for this wing-ding, I say let them eat … *(Strikes a regal pose.)* wedding cake! *(Exits downstage left hallway door. Sound effects: Loud voices from "downstairs.")*
DEEDRA. And aren't we all glad she didn't put that costume on until today?
CHARLIE. Sounds like they're having some big time down there.
DEEDRA. *(Crosses to makeup mirror, checks her appearance.)* It's probably Jamison. The man can mesmerize *any* crowd with a story. Oh, I'm so lucky!
LIBBY RUTH. Well, I think Jamison's the lucky one. You know what they say, a good lawyer knows the law, but a great lawyer knows *the judge. (They laugh.)*
DEEDRA. And he loves to travel, speaks fluent French and is *so* well-connected. When we started dating, I was shocked to find out we were a topic of gossip in legal circles all over D.C. After working so long to build a sane and serious career … *I liked it!* Which is why it's only right for this wedding to be nothing but f-u-n!
CHARLIE. And nothing says *good times* like a room full of lawyers, judges and politicians. *(Just then, Monette opens the downstage left hallway door. Sound effects: Loud voices, angry shouts from "downstairs." She enters, wild-eyed.)*

DEEDRA. Is everyone having a good time?
LIBBY RUTH. Where's Sedalia? Should we start lining up without her?
MONETTE. *(Pants.)* Wait. *(Gasps for breath, then:)* You have no idea how hard it is to run upstairs in a dress the size of a double-wide.
CHARLIE. Did you get the garter?
MONETTE. I couldn't find Kari anywhere, but we've got a bigger problem right this minute! Deedra, brace yourself: Harris is here.
DEEDRA. *(Alarmed.)* What do you mean Harris is — How is that possible?! You're saying he drove all the way here from D.C.? Why?!
MONETTE. Because he just announced to the entire room he's here to stop your wedding. *And* he's demanding you come down and speak to him.
DEEDRA. What?!
MONETTE. And you'd better hustle. Based on my years of personal experience with bar fights, I'm telling you, he and Jamison are about to come to blows.
CHARLIE. Okay, real quick here: Just off the top of your heads, do you think I carry around some kind of screwed up karma that makes things at weddings go all split-brain crazy like this?
DEEDRA. *(Steamed.)* Oh, no! He's not doing this! Harris Wingate, Mr. Nice-Guy-I'll-Do-Anything-To-Make-You-Happy-If-You'll-Just-Forgive-Me, will *not* ruin my wedding! *(Deedra storms out downstage left hallway door.)*
MONETTE. *(Calls.)* I'll go with you! You're not facing this revolution alone.
LIBBY RUTH. *(Starts for the door.)* Me, too! I need to find Kari!
CHARLIE. *(Stops them.)* Y'all can't leave me here alone! If Sedalia comes in and finds me, that grudge-bearing Southern belle's gonna ring my chimes!
MONETTE. Uh … good point.
LIBBY RUTH. *(Anger rising.)* Alright, fine! *(Fumes.)* This is just great — no garter from Kari, fistfight for Deedra. Can't we have just *one* wedding that doesn't turn into some big honkin' drama?
CHARLIE. If it involves the four of *us,* I'd say the chances are slim to none.
LIBBY RUTH. *(Oblivious, paces.)* And now Kari's had *another* disagreement with *another* young man.
MONETTE. She's spirited and has a mind of her own. So what if she did?

LIBBY RUTH. *(Steam builds.)* It *matters* because it's a pattern. Kari can't last with a boyfriend. The one she just broke up with, the architect I found for her — and believe me, that wasn't easy — was perfect. This can't keep happening!
MONETTE. Libby Ruth, everyone's on edge today. Just calm down! We don't need you to be working yourself up into one of your nervous fits!
LIBBY RUTH. *(Hasn't heard a word.)* Maybe I'm to blame for all this. Why didn't I pay closer attention? There's got to be a way I can convince her to give a guy a chance! Oh, I deserve a kick in the pants! *(Frustration builds as she attempts and fails to kick herself first with one heel, then the other.)*
CHARLIE. Okay, this is way too weird. You've gotta stop! Come on, now. I mean it. We've had enough trouble with *Monette Antoinette* today, we can't handle you cracking up on us! Now, cut it out!
LIBBY RUTH. *(Ignores Charlie, paces nervously, rattles.)* I know I'm right about this! — I've failed her, that's what I've done. It's my fault my daughter keeps sabotaging her chance at romance. And it's worrying me to death! The whole thing just makes me so tense I think my head's going to explode! *(Charlie and Monette exchange a look, grab pillows off sofa, sneak up behind Libby Ruth.)* I mean, maybe I'm just not a good mother. — And now Kari thinks she'll always be alone and I should've — *(Suddenly, WHAP! Charlie wallops Libby Ruth across her back with a pillow. Libby Ruth whirls around, startled, then Monette whaps her with a pillow again and again. Libby Ruth yelps and runs. Monette and Charlie chase her around the sofa, catch her, then pummel her with the pillows.)* What on earth are you doing?! *(They stop.)*
CHARLIE. We were trying to snap you out of it.
MONETTE. Yeah, we wanted to take you by surprise. You know, like you do when a person gets the hiccups. And, look, it worked!
CHARLIE. You don't have to thank us.
LIBBY RUTH. Believe me, the thought *never* entered my mind. *(Deedra flies in downstage left hallway door.)*
DEEDRA. It's absolute chaos down there! You've *never* seen anything like it — men in tuxedos brawling among candelabra, orchids and linen tablecloths.
MONETTE. Whoa! If they were only doing it in *kilts,* that would fulfill *two* of my *favorite* fantasies.
CHARLIE. Oh man, in front of all those politicians and lawyers.

You must be so embarassed, Deedra.
DEEDRA. Embarrassed? I'm *thrilled! (Off the others' surprise.)* Never, *ever* in my life have two men fought over me. I'm rather impressed with myself right now. *(Off their looks.)* Don't get me wrong, I'm excited about the new life Jamison and I can have together. On the other hand, I'm deeply touched that Harris is doing something so enormously out of character because he's still in love with me.
LIBBY RUTH. It's so *romantic! (Sniffs.)* Oh, no! I'm going to cry!
DEEDRA. But now I'm worried about him. Harris doesn't know what to do in a fistfight.
MONETTE. Then he'd better catch on quick, because it sounds like Jamison's just about to tear down his shack!
DEEDRA. You all know how I've wrestled with my decision to move on. But now Harris is downstairs humiliating himself in front of his peers and ruining his reputation, begging me — here, today — to give him another chance. Am I really cold enough to turn my back on him? *(Beat. Then, rapid-fire:)*
LIBBY RUTH. Well, I'd say you are, yes.
MONETTE. Shug, you could freeze a cup of coffee just sticking your finger in it.
CHARLIE. I agree. You have what I'd call a reptilian type of warmth.
DEEDRA. *(Snaps.)* It was a rhetorical question!
LIBBY RUTH. *(Takes Deedra's hand.)* Darlin', someone wise once said, "the course of true love never does run smooth." It was Shakespeare … or maybe Jackie Collins. Anyway, one of those great writers said it. My point is, if you're *not sure,* then you're going to have to do something about it and you're going to have to do it *now! (Just then, Sedalia races in downstage left hallway door. Charlie grabs her feather duster, turns her back to hide her face, dusts upstage center chest.)*
SEDALIA. Okay girls, here's the latest ringside update: Jamison bloodied Harris' nose and by the sound of the crack, I think it's broken —
LIBBY RUTH/MONETTE/DEEDRA. *(Grimace.)* Oooh …
SEDALIA. … Then Harris clubbed him over the head with a cheese board and —
LIBBY RUTH/MONETTE/DEEDRA. *(Grimace.)* Ohhh …
SEDALIA. The crowd went wild and is cheering them on! *(To Deedra.)* It's quite a duel being fought over you, madame. But on the plus

side, it *is* very French, very thematic. *(Sound effects: Breaking glass.)*
MONETTE. And is going to cost you beaucoup bucks, baby!
SEDALIA. Oh, and Libby Ruth, I want you to know, when the fight broke out, I went to the pantry to find my axe and … *your* daughter and *my* nephew were there … together … locked in a passionate kiss.
LIBBY RUTH. *(Shocked.) My* Kari and *your* Todd? Are you sure? I thought they spent the day arguing.
SEDALIA. They did. But it would seem they've … reached an *understanding. (Unseen by the others, Libby Ruth does a joyous "victory pump.")*
LIBBY RUTH. *(To herself.)* Yes!!!
SEDALIA. I've gotta say, you women do have the most *interesting* weddings. *(Notices Charlie, crosses to her.)* Excuse me, hon, I got no problem with the bride bringing you in to help out tonight, but you really don't have to dust. Just handle the — *(Takes Charlie's shoulder, turns her around. Incensed.)* It's *you*!
CHARLIE. *(Quickly moves away.)* Hey, great to see you again, Sedalia. Love the beret! *(Races out downstage left hallway door.)*
SEDALIA. *(Fumes.)* It's all making sense now! *Of course* we have a disaster on our hands — Charlie Collins is here! *(Races out downstage left hallway door after Charlie. Then, sound effects: a Crash!)*
DEEDRA. That does it! I'm putting a stop to this. Come on, girls, I need back up. *(Starts for downstage left hallway door.)*
MONETTE. You've got it, sister. Anyone gets in our way, *heads will roll!*
LIBBY RUTH. But what're you going to do?
DEEDRA. I'm going to have a wedding! I've overpaid for one and I'm having it!
MONETTE. But who are you going to marry?
DEEDRA. The last man standing! *(Flies out downstage left hallway door.)*
LIBBY RUTH. Wow! Can you believe Deedra's got *two* men after her?!
MONETTE. Well, that *is* my *ultimate* fantasy — having two men at once.
LIBBY. *(Shocked.)* What?!
MONETTE. Yep! One cookin', one cleanin'! *(They laugh, slap high fives, race out downstage left hallway door. Blackout.)*

Scene 2

A light comes up downstage right. Kari Ames-Bissette, now exuberantly tipsy, stands with her back to the audience as she continues the speech to her wedding guests she began in Act One, Scene 1.

KARI. Whoo-oooo! Know what? I think champagne might be my new favorite drink of — Wait. Am I in the right room? I was just … *(Glances over her shoulder, turns around.)* Oh, *that's* where you went! Well, aren't you a bunch of sneaky-Pete's? Anyway, I was just about to say I am so in love with each and every one of you right now. Hey, wouldn't it be great if we could all get married together to each other? *(Beat.)* Okay, maybe not. But it's *so* great to be here with all my loved ones and I mean that with all sinceriousness. And to see Aunt Viola and Uncle Huell smooching over by the punch bowl just warms my heart. So, before I floor the turn over to Todd, I'd like to say one final thingy: all my life I've admired the way my mom and godmothers have hung together and supported each other wedding after wedding after wedding. It was only logical that I chose them to be *my* bridesmaids, too. When I look at them, I tell myself, "I'm the luckiest world in the whole wide girl." So raise a glass to those loving, strong and classy women: *(Holds up her glass.)* Knockers high, girls! You'll always be the wings beneath my wind! … *(Drains her glass. Cross fade, lights down on Kari. Lights up center stage on the upstairs sitting room at Laurelton Oaks. It's a snowy winter afternoon, a little more than one year after the previous wedding, about twenty minutes before Kari's own wedding begins. Floral arrangements have changed, a pretty coffee urn, china cups and saucers, trays of cookies and finger food, a bridal bouquet and corsage in a box are on upstage center chest. An umbrella stand sits beside downstage left hallway door. Otherwise, the room has remained the same. Charlie staggers through upstage right dressing room door, in a beautiful, floor length lavender gown, a strand of pearls at her neck, white corsage on her shoulder. Badly hungover and wearing sunglasses, she struggles to coffee urn, draws a cup of coffee, guzzles it.)*

CHARLIE. *(Loud.)* Deedra, one question: What the heck did that bartender put in our drinks last night? *(Deedra, also hungover, in sunglasses, dressed identically, carrying a coffee cup, painfully enters upstage left dressing room door.)*
DEEDRA. My guess would be something from the nuclear waste family. *(Draws a cup of coffee, guzzles it. Stares at Charlie.)* Good God, that dress looks familiar.
CHARLIE. *(Gets more coffee.)* It should. You're wearing one just like it.
DEEDRA. *(Studies her own dress, gasps.)* And yet I have no memory of putting this on. *(Looks down the neck of the dress.)* Well, at least the bra's facing the right direction — that's always a good sign. *(They hold their heads, cross to sofa, sit.)*
CHARLIE. Look, there's one thing for sure, we threw Kari a great bachelorette party. *(Then, suspiciously.)* We did, didn't we?
DEEDRA. Beats me. Last thing I remember was the bartender saying "this is the hottest new drink on the menu." After the first one, everything else is a blur.
CHARLIE. At least you remember *that*. I've got nothin' after Round Two of Tequila Bingo.
DEEDRA. *(Drains the cup.)* Hey, I think the coffee's helping. Brother, it's been a year since I've felt this woozy.
CHARLIE. It's been a *year* since the cops showed up at your wedding?!
DEEDRA. And I choose to think it takes a real woman to admit she was knocked out cold during a brawl at her own nuptials.
CHARLIE. Who knew Sedalia could pack that kind of punch?! And I *still* maintain she was aiming for me. Man, that was some shindig.
DEEDRA. My favorite wedding ever! And wasn't it perfect that Harris and I came to just long enough to exchange our vows before the ambulance got here? Libby Ruth even thought *that* was romantic.
CHARLIE. She would. And you're sticking with the story that re-marrying Harris was the right choice? Come on, not even one regret?
DEEDRA. Nope. Outside the courtroom, it's the best decision I ever made. When I saw him lying there on the floor, his jacket ripped to shreds, groom's cake smashed in his hair, I knew I couldn't bear to live another day without him.

CHARLIE. I may throw up.
DEEDRA. Well, I admit it's mushy, but isn't that a little harsh?
CHARLIE. I meant from this hangover … no, wait. You're right. It's your lovey-dovey stuff that's making me nauseous. *(Sedalia hurries in downstage left hallway door in another beautiful caftan, pearls, carries a coffee carafe.)*
SEDALIA. *(Pours coffee into the urn, straightens buffet items.)* Fresh coffee, y'all. Two, three pots of this "go juice" should get you over last night's hijinks. Who knew you two were so into dirty dancing?! *(Chuckles.)* And that was one helluva fight you put up when the bouncer tried to drag you off the dance floor. *(Charlie and Deedra look at each other, horrified.)* Oh, and I need to thank you, Charlie. On your recommendation, the Trustees of the Botanical Garden booked a big symposium here at Laurelton Oaks. It'll be a nice, little feather in our cap.
DEEDRA. *(Low, to Charlie.)* So, *that's* how you wormed your way back into her good graces.
CHARLIE. *(Low.)* Money talks, baby! *(Sedalia sails across the room with a tray.)*
SEDALIA. Now, here's my sure-fire cure for a hangover — soft boiled eggs with anchovy mayonnaise — a real picker-upper. Enjoy! *(Hands the tray to Charlie, exits downstage left hallway door. Charlie and Deedra, nauseated, cringe.)*
DEEDRA. I don't care what she says, that woman's still out to get you. *(Libby Ruth hurries in downstage left hallway door. She's in an identical lavender gown, her corsage made of pink roses.)*
LIBBY RUTH. This is so romantic! Everything is just beautiful downstairs!
DEEDRA. Yes, you and Sedalia have done a wonderful job. *(Holds her head.)* And everything would be even *more* beautiful if you'd lower your voice just a decibel or two. *(Libby Ruth crosses downstage, gazes out "the window.")*
LIBBY RUTH. Well, I've learned so much working with Sedalia. And we were both determined to make this wedding perfect in every way. Look, it's almost like we planned the weather, too! The snow is so soft and pretty, just the right touch. *(To the others.)* Come look! *(Pulls them to "the window.")* But y'all can't appreciate it if you can't see it. *(Whips off their sunglasses.)* There! Isn't it lovely? *(Deedra and Charlie are blinded by the glare. They groan, cover their eyes.)*
CHARLIE. Geez, when did they start making snow so *bright?!*

LIBBY RUTH. Now all I've got to do is keep Preston, *Mr. I'm-The-Big-Strong-Daddy-Of-The-Bride,* from sobbing through the ceremony and find out where the heck Monette is. *(Checks her watch.)* I've got her dress ready to go. Have either of you heard from her?
DEEDRA. Not a peep. And it isn't like Monette to *not* notify us of every single thought she has or move she makes. Which brings up another point that's still cloudy — Monette not making it to the party. What's that about? She's looked forward to it for months.
CHARLIE. I suspect she and Gavin may have had a *disagreement.* All he said in his message last night was she wasn't going to be able to make it.
DEEDRA. Well, this *is* the longest marriage Monette's had. Traditionally, it's *way* past time for her to screw it up.
LIBBY RUTH. Let's not hit the panic button yet. I'm sure everything's fine. *(Takes in the room.)* Gosh, we've all waited for this day forever, haven't we? Funny, but I'd swear it was just yesterday Kari was the flower girl in Monette's second wedding. *(Wipes away a tear, then happily.)* Oh, I promise I'm not going to get emotional. We are going to have a big time today! *(Then, merrily.)* And you certainly set the right tone when you and that hunky busboy danced the cha-cha *on* the bar last night, Deedra! *(Crosses downstage to dressing table, checks her makeup. Deedra staggers, mortified. Charlie steadies her.)*
DEEDRA. *(Low, to Charlie.)* As God is my witness, nothing stronger than *milk* will ever pass these lips again! *(Libby Ruth's cell phone rings offstage.)*
LIBBY RUTH. Please let that be Monette! *(Runs out upstage left dressing room door.)*
CHARLIE. I had no idea you knew how to do the cha-cha.
DEEDRA. Neither did I.
CHARLIE. That party must've been a whole lot wilder than we thought.
DEEDRA. But by some miracle we still managed to get here and into these outfits. I think we look pretty good in spite of ourselves. You must agree since I haven't heard any of your usual complaints about being shoved into another bridesmaid dress.
CHARLIE. That's because I figured out a way to make it work for me. *And* I'm ready for my date at the indoor putting green after the reception.
DEEDRA. Get serious! You can't play golf in a dress.

CHARLIE. Of course not! *(Raises her skirt. Plaid golf shorts are underneath it.)* Throw on a polo shirt, my cleats, I am good to go.
DEEDRA. Well, I guess what really matters is that we're all doing whatever it takes to make us happy. Here's to our *fabulous fifties!*
CHARLIE. And may Monette enjoy *hers* — seven to ten years from now! *(They chuckle, touch coffee cups. Libby Ruth races in upstage left dressing room door.)*
LIBBY RUTH. That was *Gavin!* Now I know what happened: Monette broke her foot on the way to the party and ended up in the Emergency Room. They reset a bone and now they're keeping her in the hospital overnight.
DEEDRA. That's terrible! Is she alright?
CHARLIE. And how on earth did she manage to break her foot?
LIBBY RUTH. Gavin says Monette's fine, just mad as a hornet she can't get here for the wedding. And she broke it when — get this — she was at Walgreen's, reaching up to get a pair of false eyelashes when *she fell off her five inch heels!*
DEEDRA. Revenge of the killer stilettos!
CHARLIE. Poor ol' Monette. I'm sorry she'll miss the ceremony.
LIBBY RUTH. *(Idea!)* But that's *all* she's gonna miss! I say, after the reception, let's carry some wedding cake to her and Gavin at the hospital.
DEEDRA. Perfect! Cancel your date, Charlie. We're taking the party to our fallen comrade.
LIBBY RUTH. Deedra, would you mind breaking the news about Monette to Kari? If I try, it'll push me over the brink and I'll be as big a mess as Preston.
DEEDRA. Sure. I'll take one for the team. *(Exits into upstage right dressing room.)*
LIBBY RUTH. *(A sobering thought.)* Wow, you realize this is the first time we'll be bridesmaids with one of us missing? *(Then, rallies.)* Well, we'll have to readjust some things. Now I have to find my … *(Looks around.)* uh … my … well, *that's* gone. Shoot. I can't remember diddly.
CHARLIE. What's wrong?
LIBBY RUTH. Getting older. It's not fair! I can't hold a thought, but I can *still* retain water! *(Deedra enters from upstage right dressing room door.)*
DEEDRA. She took it like a champ. That goddaughter of ours is strong *and* beautiful! *(Checks her watch.)* Okay, girls, we've got to

go downstairs *now.*
LIBBY RUTH. Oh, my gosh! It's *time? (Just then, Monette, in a heavy coat and a walking cast on one foot, hospital slipper on the other, a string mop for a crutch, opens downstage left hallway door. Lipstick smeared across her face, her hair's a mess, she's a wreck.)*
MONETTE. Dang straight, it's *time*! Time to HELP ME! I've got to get ready for this hullabaloo! *(The others run to her.)*
LIBBY RUTH. Monette, what're you doing here?!
DEEDRA. My gosh, she's bleeding! Get her to the sofa before she faints!
MONETTE. I'm not *bleeding!* I was *trying* to put on lipstick when the cabbie hit a snow bank and knocked me into the floor. Who's got a tissue?
LIBBY RUTH. *(Hands her one.)* So, is Gavin with you?
MONETTE. No! He doesn't even know I escaped. That man was hovering over me like an old maid aunt. And my doctor was tied up all day with emergencies and they wouldn't release me 'til he got there. So when Gavin went out for coffee, I made a run for it … okay, a *hobble* for it. Now, get me into my dress before they come after me! I *will* be in this wedding.
LIBBY RUTH. You are wonderful, Monette. *(Kisses her cheek, runs out upstage left dressing room door.)*
CHARLIE. She's right. I mean, you *do* look like an escapee from the nut farm but you're one helluva friend.
MONETTE. *(Sweetly.)* Thanks. I think the same thing about you, too. *(Deedra and Charlie get Monette's coat off to reveal she's in a hospital gown. Libby Ruth returns with Monette's matching bridesmaid dress.)*
LIBBY RUTH. Uh, oh. You're missing a few foundation garments. I could go look for some.
DEEDRA. There's no time! Sorry, Monette, but this dress is going on over the hospital gown. *(She and Charlie wrestle the dress onto Monette. During the following, the three women dress Monette, clean her up and get her presentable.)*
CHARLIE. Don't worry about it. She's an old hand at wearing no underwear in front of a crowd, right, Monette?
MONETTE. Will you *stop* bringing that up?! *(Then.)* Wait a minute! Didn't you bring my heels over here with the dress?
LIBBY RUTH. You're in a walking cast. You're not wearing high heels tonight!
DEEDRA. Or *ever* again! We've been telling you for years to give

up those ridiculously-high heels, surely you've learned your lesson! After you turn thirty, with each successive decade, you *have* to buy heels that are one inch shorter.
MONETTE. *(Wails!)* Noooo! Life won't be worth living. Not getting to wear my five-inchers will kill me! And I tell you one thing for sure, this stupid foot had *better* heal in two months. Gavin and I are going to San Francisco to celebrate our seventh wedding anniversary.
LIBBY RUTH. San Francisco? I thought you wanted to go to London.
MONETTE. I did, but there's a special class at the Culinary Institute in Napa Gavin wants to take, so I rebooked everything. It's not all about *me,* you know. *(The others stare at her in disbelief.)*
DEEDRA. *(To Charlie and Libby Ruth.)* She really *did* say that, right?
CHARLIE. She did. Monette actually thought of somebody else first. They are ice skating in Hades as we speak.
MONETTE. So what if I've changed my tune? This is the longest relationship I've *ever* had. Can you believe someone would stay with me *seven whole years?*
CHARLIE. I certainly can't. It's been all *we* could do to stick with you as long as *we* have. *(Libby Ruth pinches Charlie, pins corsage on Monette. Sedalia sticks her head in downstage left hallway door.)*
SEDALIA. Two minute warning, girls. *(Sees Monette.)* Oh, great! You made it after all. I'll tell the harpist to pluck slower so you can get ready.
MONETTE. I *am* ready.
SEDALIA. Oh. Then I'll tell the harpist to pluck slower so you can take another crack at it. *(Exits.)*
CHARLIE. I tell you what, even *without* the axe, *that* woman is one scary mama! *(Kari enters from upstage right dressing room in her wedding gown and veil, carries a beautiful bouquet.)*
KARI. Honestly, y'all. Wouldn't this be a lot more fun if we were in jeans and sweatshirts?
MONETTE. Oh, my stars! You are one gorgeous bride!
KARI. *(Squeals, runs to her.)* Monette, you made it! Thank you, thank you … but … are you okay?
MONETTE. Of course I am. No goddaughter of mine's going to tie the knot without me watching her seal the deal. *(They hug.)*
LIBBY RUTH. Oh, isn't she the prettiest thing you've ever seen?

I mean picture perfect! How could anyone — Wait a minute! Your hem isn't right! There's a little puck right there! *(Drops to her knees, inspects hem.)* I can't let you walk down the aisle with a puck showin'! Does anyone have safety pins? I'll even take duct tape. Charlie, go tell Sedalia to stop the wedding, I've got to redo—

KARI. Mom, the ship has sailed! *(To the others.)* Y'all help me! If she keeps this up, she'll have me stripped naked and that's not supposed to happen until way later tonight! *(Deedra and Charlie pull Libby Ruth away.)*

DEEDRA. She's fine, Libby Ruth. You've got to let go, girlfriend. *(Sedalia sticks her head in downstage left hallway door.)*

SEDALIA. Places, ladies. *(Spots Kari, crosses to her.)* Oh, my dear, you are lovely! My nephew is certainly a lucky young man!

LIBBY RUTH. *(To Sedalia.)* Aren't you sweet? And now that we'll be related, I bet you'll insist on giving us a very generous family discount on this wedding.

SEDALIA. *(Laughs.)* Family discount? Oh, Libby Ruth, you are such a cut-up! *(Laughs harder.)* Family discount! That kills me! *(Exits. Libby Ruth shrugs it off, arranges Kari's veil.)*

CHARLIE. Alright, girls, let's fall in line.

KARI. Well … I guess this is it. *(Beat. Everyone realizes this is the moment. Libby Ruth and Kari embrace.)*

LIBBY RUTH. *(Pulls back. Rallies.)* Okay, let's get our baby girl married! *(Everyone starts toward the door.)*

MONETTE. STOP!! *(Hobbles to dressing table, checks her makeup.)* Okay, I'm gorgeous! *Now* we can go!

KARI. Ooh! My stomach just did a flip-flop! I think I'm more nervous about giving my speech at the reception than getting through the ceremony. Oh, and *please* make sure nobody gives me any champagne. I can't handle it. One glass and I'll start blathering like a fool.

DEEDRA. Don't be silly! You'd *never* do that in front of your guests.

KARI. *(Deep breath.)* Alright then, I'm ready. *(Pecks Libby Ruth's cheek.)* Thank you. *(They share a moment. Libby Ruth runs to downstage left hallway door, opens it.)*

LIBBY RUTH. Alright! Here goes the bride! *(Kari leads the way, exits. From this point, the pace slows, the women savor each moment. Then.)* Well, look at us. We made a vow to be in each others' weddings almost forty years ago … and we did it.

CHARLIE. And against *all* odds. Not too shabby for four little girls who couldn't even get dates to the prom.
DEEDRA. And we've gotten so good at it, now we're farming ourselves out to the next generation.
CHARLIE. Know what? Men have come and gone over the years, but y'all have always been there for me. It's meant everything to me.
MONETTE. Yeah, people are lucky if they have just one friend for life, but look at us, we've each got three. *(They hug.)*
DEEDRA. We've got a lot to celebrate, girls, not the least of which is that this is the last time we're going to be bridesmaids!
LIBBY RUTH. *(Mischievous.)* Or is it? Didn't I hear Deedra say you have a date, Charlie? So, what's going on? Someone we should know about? Any chance you might take another shot at the old altar?
CHARLIE. *(Takes her by the shoulders.)* Woman, pay attention: I have slammed that door and nailed the sucker shut. I've realized I like my life. I enjoy going out with any guy I want to. I'm happy! Not everybody *has* to be married to feel "complete." People are always sayin' you can't live without love. Personally, I think oxygen and Reese's Pieces are far more essential but, hey, that's just me.
LIBBY RUTH. Well, you can't be too sure.
CHARLIE. Nope. I'm sure.
DEEDRA. Still and all, you never know.
CHARLIE. Actually, I *do* know. I'm done!
MONETTE. Trust me, never say never!
CHARLIE. Never, never, never, never, never, never, never, *never!*
LIBBY RUTH. We're just saying, it's something to think about.
CHARLIE. I've already thought about it. *Now* my goal is to die on my one hundredth birthday in my beach house in Tahiti. And I want my boyfriend to be so upset he'll have to drop out of college! *(Exits upstage left hallway door. Deedra throws her hands up in mock exasperation, exits upstage left hallway door. Libby Ruth stops Monette.)*
LIBBY RUTH. *(Conspiratorially, low.)* I still say, where there's a date, there's hope.
MONETTE. *(Kisses Libby Ruth's forehead.)* Hold that positive thought, darlin'. *(Hobbles out upstage left hallway door.)*
LIBBY RUTH. *(At upstage left hallway door, turns back toward the room, sighs. Then, to herself.)* Oh, this is all *so* romantic! *(Can't help*

herself, starts to sing terribly off-key.) AH, SWEET MYSTERY OF LIFE AT LAST I'VE — *(Deedra reaches in the door, grabs Libby Ruth's arm, yanks her out the door. Blackout.)*

End of Play

PROPERTY LIST

Champagne flutes (6)
Champagne bottle
Make-up
Shopping bags
Large purse
Iron/ironing board
Spray bottle
Business card
Tissues/tissue box
Hairbrush
Lysol
Cleaning cloth
Comb
Hair ribbon
Misc. fabric re: Deedra's outfit
Bridal bouquets (3)
Nosegays (3)
Coin
Tray of snacks, pickles, etc.
Corsage boxes (3)
Corsages (3)
Oversized axe
Champagne bucket
Cell phone
Stuffed toy poodle
Lace fan
Feather duster
Drawstring purse (reticule)
Driver's license
Tray of macaroons
Coffee urn
China coffee cups
Tray of cookies
Coffee carafe
Tray of soft-boiled eggs

SOUND EFFECTS

Cell phone ring
Thunder
Loud voices
Breaking glass
A crash

NEW PLAYS

★ **MOTHERS AND SONS by Terrence McNally.** At turns funny and powerful, MOTHERS AND SONS portrays a woman who pays an unexpected visit to the New York apartment of her late son's partner, who is now married to another man and has a young son. Challenged to face how society has changed around her, generations collide as she revisits the past and begins to see the life her son might have led. "A resonant elegy for a ravaged generation." –NY Times. "A moving reflection on a changed America." –Chicago Tribune. [2M, 1W, 1 boy] ISBN: 978-0-8222-3183-7

★ **THE HEIR APPARENT by David Ives, adapted from Le Légataire Universel by Jean-François Regnard.** Paris, 1708. Eraste, a worthy though penniless young man, is in love with the fair Isabelle, but her forbidding mother, Madame Argante, will only let the two marry if Eraste can show he will inherit the estate of his rich but miserly Uncle Geronte. Unfortunately, old Geronte has also fallen for the fair Isabelle, and plans to marry her this very day and leave her everything in his will—separating the two young lovers forever. Eraste's wily servant Crispin jumps in, getting a couple of meddling relatives disinherited by impersonating them (one, a brash American, the other a French female country cousin)—only to have the old man kick off before his will is made! In a brilliant stroke, Crispin then impersonates the old man, dictating a will favorable to his master (and Crispin himself, of course)—only to find that rich Uncle Geronte isn't dead at all and is more than ever ready to marry Isabelle! The multiple strands of the plot are unraveled to great comic effect in the streaming rhyming couplets of French classical comedy, and everyone lives happily, and richly, ever after. [4M, 3W] ISBN: 978-0-8222-2808-0

★ **HANDLE WITH CARE by Jason Odell Williams.** Circumstances both hilarious and tragic bring together a young Israeli woman, who has little command of English, and a young American man, who has little command of romance. Is their inevitable love an accident…or is it destiny, generations in the making? "A hilarious and heartwarming romantic comedy." –NY Times. "Hilariously funny! Utterly charming, fearlessly adorable and a tiny bit magical." –Naples News. [2M, 2W] ISBN: 978-0-8222-3138-7

★ **LAST GAS by John Cariani.** Nat Paradis is a Red Sox-loving part-time dad who manages Paradis' Last Convenient Store, the last convenient place to get gas—or anything—before the Canadian border to the north and the North Maine Woods to the west. When an old flame returns to town, Nat gets a chance to rekindle a romance he gave up on years ago. But sparks fly as he's forced to choose between new love and old. "Peppered with poignant characters [and] sharp writing." –Portland Phoenix. "Very funny and surprisingly thought-provoking." –Portland Press Herald. [4M, 3W] ISBN: 978-0-8222-3232-2

DRAMATISTS PLAY SERVICE, INC.
440 Park Avenue South, New York, NY 10016 212-683-8960 Fax 212-213-1539
postmaster@dramatists.com www.dramatists.com

NEW PLAYS

★ **ACT ONE by James Lapine.** Growing up in an impoverished Bronx family and forced to drop out of school at age thirteen, Moss Hart dreamed of joining the glamorous world of the theater. Hart's famous memoir *Act One* plots his unlikely collaboration with the legendary playwright George S. Kaufman and his arrival on Broadway. Tony Award-winning writer and director James Lapine has adapted Act One for the stage, creating a funny, heartbreaking and suspenseful celebration of a playwright and his work. "…brims contagiously with the ineffable, irrational and irrefutable passion for that endangered religion called the Theater." –NY Times. "…wrought with abundant skill and empathy." –Time Out. [8M, 4W] ISBN: 978-0-8222-3217-9

★ **THE VEIL by Conor McPherson.** May 1822, rural Ireland. The defrocked Reverend Berkeley arrives at the crumbling former glory of Mount Prospect House to accompany a young woman to England. Seventeen-year-old Hannah is to be married off to a marquis in order to resolve the debts of her mother's estate. However, compelled by the strange voices that haunt his beautiful young charge and a fascination with the psychic current that pervades the house, Berkeley proposes a séance, the consequences of which are catastrophic. "…an effective mixture of dark comedy and suspense." –Telegraph (London). "A cracking fireside tale of haunting and decay." –Times (London). [3M, 5W] ISBN: 978-0-8222-3313-8

★ **AN OCTOROON by Branden Jacobs-Jenkins. Winner of the 2014 OBIE Award for Best New American Play.** Judge Peyton is dead and his plantation Terrebonne is in financial ruins. Peyton's handsome nephew George arrives as heir apparent and quickly falls in love with Zoe, a beautiful octoroon. But the evil overseer M'Closky has other plans—for both Terrebonne and Zoe. In 1859, a famous Irishman wrote this play about slavery in America. Now an American tries to write his own. "AN OCTOROON invites us to laugh loudly and easily at how naïve the old stereotypes now seem, until nothing seems funny at all." –NY Times [10M, 5W] ISBN: 978-0-8222-3226-1

★ **IVANOV translated and adapted by Curt Columbus.** In this fascinating early work by Anton Chekhov, we see the union of humor and pathos that would become his trademark. A restless man, Nicholai Ivanov struggles to dig himself out of debt and out of provincial boredom. When the local doctor, Lvov, informs Ivanov that his wife Anna is dying and accuses him of worsening her condition with his foul moods, Ivanov is sent into a downward spiral of depression and ennui. He soon finds himself drawn to a beautiful young woman, Sasha, full of hope and energy. Finding himself stuck between a romantic young mistress and his ailing wife, Ivanov falls deeper into crisis, heading toward inevitable tragedy. [8M, 8W] ISBN: 978-0-8222-3155-4

DRAMATISTS PLAY SERVICE, INC.
440 Park Avenue South, New York, NY 10016 212-683-8960 Fax 212-213-1539
postmaster@dramatists.com www.dramatists.com

NEW PLAYS

★ **I'LL EAT YOU LAST: A CHAT WITH SUE MENGERS by John Logan.** For more than 20 years, Sue Mengers' clients were the biggest names in show business: Barbra Streisand, Faye Dunaway, Burt Reynolds, Ali MacGraw, Gene Hackman, Cher, Candice Bergen, Ryan O'Neal, Nick Nolte, Mike Nichols, Gore Vidal, Bob Fosse…If her clients were the talk of the town, she was the town, and her dinner parties were the envy of Hollywood. Now, you're invited into her glamorous Beverly Hills home for an evening of dish, dirty secrets and all the inside showbiz details only Sue can tell you. "A delectable soufflé of a solo show…thanks to the buoyant, witty writing of Mr. Logan" –NY Times. "80 irresistible minutes of primo tinseltown dish from a certified master chef." –Hollywood Reporter. [1W] ISBN: 978-0-8222-3079-3

★ **PUNK ROCK by Simon Stephens.** In a private school outside of Manchester, England, a group of highly-articulate seventeen-year-olds flirt and posture their way through the day while preparing for their A-Level mock exams. With hormones raging and minimal adult supervision, the students must prepare for their future — and survive the savagery of high school. Inspired by playwright Simon Stephens' own experiences as a teacher, PUNK ROCK is an honest and unnerving chronicle of contemporary adolescence. "[A] tender, ferocious and frightning play." –NY Times. "[A] muscular little play that starts out funny and ferocious then reveals its compassion by degrees." –Hollywood Reporter. [5M, 3W] ISBN: 978-0-8222-3288-9

★ **THE COUNTRY HOUSE by Donald Margulies.** A brood of famous and longing-to-be-famous creative artists have gathered at their summer home during the Williamstown Theatre Festival. When the weekend takes an unexpected turn, everyone is forced to improvise, inciting a series of simmering jealousies, romantic outbursts, and passionate soul-searching. Both witty and compelling, THE COUNTRY HOUSE provides a piercing look at a family of performers coming to terms with the roles they play in each other's lives. "A valentine to the artists of the stage." –NY Times. "Remarkably candid and funny." –Variety. [3M, 3W] ISBN: 978-0-8222-3274-2

★ **OUR LADY OF KIBEHO by Katori Hall.** Based on real events, OUR LADY OF KIBEHO is an exploration of faith, doubt, and the power and consequences of both. In 1981, a village girl in Rwanda claims to see the Virgin Mary. Ostracized by her schoolmates and labeled disturbed, everyone refuses to believe, until impossible happenings appear again and again. Skepticism gives way to fear, and then to belief, causing upheaval in the school community and beyond. "Transfixing." –NY Times. "Hall's passionate play renews belief in what theater can do." –Time Out [7M, 8W, 1 boy] ISBN: 978-0-8222-3301-5

DRAMATISTS PLAY SERVICE, INC.
440 Park Avenue South, New York, NY 10016 212-683-8960 Fax 212-213-1539
postmaster@dramatists.com www.dramatists.com

NEW PLAYS

★ **AGES OF THE MOON by Sam Shepard.** Byron and Ames are old friends, reunited by mutual desperation. Over bourbon on ice, they sit, reflect and bicker until fifty years of love, friendship and rivalry are put to the test at the barrel of a gun. "A poignant and honest continuation of themes that have always been present in the work of one of this country's most important dramatists, here reconsidered in the light and shadow of time passed." –NY Times. "Finely wrought...as enjoyable and enlightening as a night spent stargazing." –Talkin' Broadway. [2M] ISBN: 978-0-8222-2462-4

★ **ALL THE WAY by Robert Schenkkan. Winner of the 2014 Tony Award for Best Play.** November, 1963. An assassin's bullet catapults Lyndon Baines Johnson into the presidency. A Shakespearean figure of towering ambition and appetite, this charismatic, conflicted Texan hurls himself into the passage of the Civil Rights Act—a tinderbox issue emblematic of a divided America—even as he campaigns for re-election in his own right, and the recognition he so desperately wants. In Pulitzer Prize and Tony Award–winning Robert Schenkkan's vivid dramatization of LBJ's first year in office, means versus ends plays out on the precipice of modern America. ALL THE WAY is a searing, enthralling exploration of the morality of power. It's not personal, it's just politics. "...action-packed, thoroughly gripping... jaw-dropping political drama." –Variety. "A theatrical coup...nonstop action. The suspense of a first-class thriller." –NY1. [17M, 3W] ISBN: 978-0-8222-3181-3

★ **CHOIR BOY by Tarell Alvin McCraney.** The Charles R. Drew Prep School for Boys is dedicated to the creation of strong, ethical black men. Pharus wants nothing more than to take his rightful place as leader of the school's legendary gospel choir. Can he find his way inside the hallowed halls of this institution if he sings in his own key? "[An] affecting and honest portrait...of a gay youth tentatively beginning to find the courage to let the truth about himself become known." –NY Times. "In his stirring and stylishly told drama, Tarell Alvin McCraney cannily explores race and sexuality and the graces and gravity of history." –NY Daily News. [7M] ISBN: 978-0-8222-3116-5

★ **THE ELECTRIC BABY by Stefanie Zadravec.** When Helen causes a car accident that kills a young man, a group of fractured souls cross paths and connect around a mysterious dying baby who glows like the moon. Folk tales and folklore weave throughout this magical story of sad endings, strange beginnings and the unlikely people that get you from one place to the next. "The imperceptible magic that pervades human existence and the power of myth to assuage sorrow are invoked by the playwright as she entwines the lives of strangers in THE ELECTRIC BABY, a touching drama." –NY Times. "As dazzling as the dialogue is dreamful." –Pittsburgh City Paper. [3M, 3W] ISBN: 978-0-8222-3011-3

DRAMATISTS PLAY SERVICE, INC.
440 Park Avenue South, New York, NY 10016 212-683-8960 Fax 212-213-1539
postmaster@dramatists.com   www.dramatists.com